Ps. 34:5

Kris

There Had Better Be a Corner!

Kris Beaird

Kris Beaird
Life Coach / Speaker
Kris.Beaird@gmail.com
www.MaxCoach.pro

Dedication and Acknowledgements

I would like to dedicate this book first of all to my mother, Idella Johanson, who passed away in 2014 at age 96. She was a courageous woman who pressed forward through tragedy to lead our family from "religion" to "relationship" with God. My greatest memory of her is that of seeing her lifting her hands in praise to God in the morning hours to gain strength from God after tragedy struck our family.

I also want to dedicate this book to my husband, Jim, of 48 years! What a journey we have been on in raising three sons, in marriage and in ministry together! He has always believed in my potential more than I did and continually encourages me to dream more! Jim is a solid rock man of God and a fun partner in life!

Where do I even begin to list the wonderful mentors in my life who have walked beside me in ministry and life? All the church "mothers" who encouraged me when I was younger and the "sisters" along the way have been priceless! I'm so grateful for growing up in a solid and fun church in Rapid City, South Dakota, where I met my spiritual mentor and mother-in-law, Dorothy Beaird. She was instrumental in helping build a firm foundation for my faith. I always said if I ever wrote a book, the title would be, "There had better be a corner!" So, here it is! I trust you are encouraged and will press forward to your corner!

There Had Better Be a Corner!

CONTENTS

FORWARD

It has been a joy to know Kris Beaird for many decades. However, it has been more recent, while partnering together in ministry, that we developed a close bond. She is truly and will always be a Forever Friend.

What a delight to watch Kris as she has morphed through many transitions. Though I've known her and about most of her experiences, I loved learning from this book about deeper layers, as she unfolded her journey of tragedy to transformation.

The catchy title of, "There Had Better Be A Corner!" sparked my interest and I could not wait to read it! Kris' gift of creatively and vulnerably communicating her story, that includes truths from God's Word, will encourage readers. Her life-story can help shine light in the darkness to those reading and bring health—emotionally, mentally, and spiritually. May it give a renewed sense of hope that could possibly be "Just Around the Corner." I'm so grateful and proud of you, Kris.

Barbara Bach

Introduction

If I heard it once, I had heard it a hundred times. "Just hang in there, Kris. Don't quit! Your victory is just around the corner," they said with assurance. It seemed like I was barely hanging on by a thread—emotionally, spiritually, and physically. Then it hit me. I really began to wonder if it was true. I had always loved and served God in ministry with my husband as youth pastors, "save-the-church" pastorates, associate pastorate, and then church planting in Colorado. My faith began to waver, even though we had weathered so much adversity already. What if it wasn't true that God had something special "just around the corner" if only we stood firm? What if this was all hype talk from our overseers designed to keep us in churches nobody else wanted to serve?

An important part of my background or "testimony" is that I'm a church-girl with no morbid story of drugs, rebellion, or promiscuousness. I just obeyed and prayed, married the preacher boy, then set out to serve God. Some of us church-girls don't feel like we even have a testimony since we didn't rebel. That's what makes my story confusing. Now that I'm "around the corner," the plan makes more sense, but in the meantime, the fog had settled in. I had never been one to question God, but before the "corner," the questions came flooding out of me:

- What if all of this was a joke?
- Have I been an idiot to believe all of this Christian stuff?
- Does everyone else see it except me?
- If God really loves me, why is this happening?
- How can I help anyone at this point in my faith? I feel helpless.
- Why do I feel so much shame? "God, you are ashamed of me as a wife, mom, and pastor's wife, aren't you? When will you be proud of me? I'm trying so hard!"
- Does God even have time for me? He says I'm special, but I don't feel special.
- I listen to my husband's dreams and support him, but what about my dreams? Can I have any? When is *my* turn?
- We're raising our three sons to trust you and fulfill their purpose in life, but what about me? I feel lost and LAST!
- As a ministry leader, I'm supposed to have the answers and now I only have questions! Am I a joke or a fake?

If you relate to any of the above, we've already made a significant connection. God took me out of the rat race of ministry, pulled me to the side of the road, and allowed me time to be restored to health and even returned the joy of my salvation. It wasn't easy or fast, but it was worth it. I promise that if you will open your heart, you will receive the same grace and spiritual nourishment necessary for you to understand God's purposes and receive a full measure of the joy He has for you.

While everyone eventually questions their faith and its daily purpose for their lives, I entered into a genuine encounter with doubt and fear that seemed to paralyze every fiber of my being. I decided to pen these thoughts and feelings in hope that others, like myself, will gain needed perspective to help them persevere through the times God designed to make them the leaders (and followers) they should be. This book chronicles the result of having made a decision to trust God even though external indicators said otherwise. I can tell you with absolute certainty that the Father does have a plan and that plan is not designed to facilitate our demise.

When a car gets a flat tire, the driver has a choice to pull over immediately for repairs or to drive until the tire is destroyed, at which time the driver is still in a dilemma. If he keeps driving on the flat, he might get further down the road, but will be in worse condition than if he'd stopped and changed the tire. When a person breaks their arm, they have a choice to go to the doctor to have the arm set in a cast for proper healing or to pretend nothing happened. I chose to use this example because some people are die-hard in their assertion that they can take care of themselves and ignore the warning signs trying to get their attention. When we ignore help, the dilemma to becomes greater. To the normal person, these natural situations seem easy to solve— get immediate help! However, in ministry, some of us keep going until we reach a breaking point and then blame God. But here's the deal: we are human, not divine! We have a body, soul, and spirit that need proper care. If we refuse or ignore those needs, the results will leak out in more dangerous ways causing damage to ourselves and to those around us—family, friends, and churches.

This book records my journey through life and ministry and how God brought me "just around the corner." While writing a book was never my dream, what He has accomplished in me is a result of learning to dream and believe the promise given to me in Habakkuk 2:1-3 in the Message Bible:

"What's God going to say to my questions? I'm braced for the worst. I'll climb to the lookout tower and scan the horizon. I'll wait to see what God says, how he'll answer my complaint. And then God answered: "Write this. Write what you see. Write it out in big block letters so that it can be read on the run. This vision-message is a witness pointing to what's coming. It aches for the coming—it can hardly wait! And it doesn't lie. If it seems slow in coming, wait. It's on its way. It will come right on time."

Are you beginning to feel hope when reading this? That's because God gives hope. I'm writing my story to help others who may be at the breaking point and asking the same questions. **GUESS WHAT? There *is* a corner and there *is* hope!** Difficult circumstances and people cloud our vision, but God really does have a plan and He really does care about your dreams. Right now, He is conforming you to His image in the middle of all your "stuff." It may be hard to believe right now, but He is fulfilling His purpose in you and it will be absolutely amazing! Trust me!

Part 1: Journey to the "Corner"

Throughout our journey, life always seems to insert detours, distractions, discouragements, times of despair, and roadblocks of fearful thought. The journey holds promise, but the problem is that many along the way have set up camp within eyesight of the highway. They watch as others struggle on to the horizon and then disappear. They wonder if they should reignite their former passion and once again press on to the place their blessing awaits—"just around the corner." Some do and some don't. Some stand erect and square their shoulders for another attempt to reach the destination. Others sit and pine away at opportunity lost. Their campsite becomes their home.

Everyone has a journey. There are no boring sagas of life lived through pressures and preconceptions. Every journey validates the individual's progress toward their promise. Every journey is designed by God to develop His child's faith that "what He promised, He will provide." Every journey, no matter how tedious or difficult, takes us closer to the blessings "just around the corner."

Chapter 1

From Tragedy to Destiny: The Story *Behind* the Story – Part 1

"If individuals find themselves trapped in a revolving platform of guilt, they usually look for a place to assign the blame so they can move on."

A person's eventual destiny originates in several "trigger" events that shape one's perspective and solidify their course in life. These events are often tragedies that cause the inventory of a person's life to be carefully evaluated in terms of future careful behavior to avoid a repeat of the devastating occurrence. If individuals find themselves trapped in a revolving platform of guilt, they usually look for a place to assign the blame so they can move on. Ironically, some people are never able to move on due to the heavy price inflicted and the recurring shockwaves emanating from the incident that changed the course of their life. It is often easiest to blame one's self and allow shame to take residency in their heart. At other times, the blame gets laid at the feet of a person perceived responsible for the tragedy. Whichever way the pendulum swings, the whole family is affected like a mobile in a baby's crib when one piece gets touched and the whole mobile starts to move.

Our family had a trigger event that changed us all forever. I intend to illustrate how good families fall victim to tragedy and become the unwilling prey of the enemy of our soul. We wanted only what every family wants—a normal life free from the reach of events that hold potential power over the healthy development of an ordinary family. Yet, as I look back now on the events as they transpired, I can see that God had his hand upon our family— just as He always promised He would.

I was born the fourth of five children in Newcastle, Wyoming in the early 1950's to a good, blue-collar family. We had our quirks and dysfunctions as every family does, but I felt loved and cared for. On the scale of family characteristics, we tipped the scale as practical and serious! My father was a hard-working immigrant from Sweden who had dreams of making it good in America. When Dad was nineteen years old, his uncle who was already in America, sponsored him to come to Montana to live and work with him. Dad's uncle was a strict enforcer of a hard day's work and would often humiliate him and use him as an "example" to the other workers to let them know he wouldn't grant any favors just because they were related. Immigrants are often hassled and taunted because they don't know English and that was the case for Dad. The first words he learned were curse words the other workers taught him. When he cursed, they all laughed because he didn't know the full import of what he was saying, and the other workers took advantage of the opportunity to make light of him. With everything and seemingly everyone against him he stayed true to his dream and worked all the harder to change the hand he had been dealt in life. That uncle would later enter politics and became the Governor of Montana, Hugo Aaronson.

Years later, knowing that the American dream was for everyone in America, Dad started his own trucking business in the oil fields of Wyoming. He left early in the morning and came home late at night after we were in bed. However, as a little girl of five or six years of age, I do remember special times of sitting with him and combing his hair while he watched television. Those were the days when we only received three channels and all telecasting ended at midnight. I remember the fuzzy lines across the small screen, and Walter Cronkite and Art Linkletter! I was a very compliant child and never received spankings while my younger brother stayed out too late playing with the neighbor kids and hardly winced at his spankings. It was worth it to him. To this day, he plays hard and works hard!

Given their financial success, my parents built a new home and were well respected in the community. They were involved in church and many of the social clubs of the small town. However, my mother was always hungry for God. She raised her hand at a main-line denominational church for salvation one day, but never heard any more about it. My older sister, Karen, would sing specials at church and then was told one day not to sing any more songs about "blood," as in the "blood of Jesus," as the church's theology began to take on a more "user friendly" quality.

My father made frequent trips to Sweden to visit his family. On this particular trip, he took my 16-year-old brother, John, with him. My oldest brother, Aaron, was in college in Arizona, my sister, Karen, at college in Wyoming, and my younger brother, Steve, and I were in grade school.

While getting ready for school one day, the phone rang. It's a phone call I will never forget even though I was only eight years old. My mother listened for a moment and then screamed, "No, no, no!" I thought something had happened to my dad and brother while traveling to Sweden. Time seemed to stop completely as we waited breathlessly to hear what had caused my mother's tormented screams. The caller said that my brother in Arizona had been in a very serious car accident with college friends.

You can only imagine the turmoil and terror that ensued from that day. My younger brother and I were taken to the neighbors for two weeks while my mother and sister flew to Arizona to be with Aaron. My father's uncle, Governor Hugo Aaronson, contacted New York's Governor Rockefeller who sent a helicopter to the ship a hundred miles offshore to bring my father back home. Dad literally climbed the rope ladder to the helicopter! Gov. Rockefeller had a plane ticket for him to fly on to Arizona to meet Mother. On the plane, Dad overheard someone say, "I hear Governor Rockefeller is on this flight."

My brother, John, continued on the ship to Sweden with plans for my father to join him later after he arrived in Sweden. However, that didn't happen. Aaron lived a few days, just long enough for my parents to arrive. My dad always told him to never ride in the car with friends. Since it was May and near the end of the semester, he rode in the back seat with friends to study for finals. On their way home, the driver lost control of the car on a gravel detour. Aaron was the only one killed. He died from a massive brain hemorrhage and never regained consciousness.

Aaron had been a senior at the University of Arizona, soon to graduate with an Electrical Engineering degree and to be engaged. During the summers, he worked with my father in the oil fields and, as the oldest child, was adored. He was in the National Guard. Since I was only eight, he had been in college and busy with high school most of my life so my interaction with him was limited. But I'll never forget the impact his death had on our family, and particularly, my mother.

The sadness that followed was intense. I remember everything about it. My parents were in a daze and Karen did her best to help them through everything. I remember the funeral, the 21-gun salute at the graveside, the friends and family, and everyone crying for what seemed like weeks and months. During pensive moments, my dad would just shake his head sadly and say, "I told him not to ride in the car with friends! I told him!"

My brother, John, stayed in Sweden with family members for several weeks until things settled down. However, by the time he returned, the funeral was over and no one wanted to talk about it anymore. In retrospect, my parents regretted that he was left to grieve alone. He too, became a victim of this trigger event and has had to deal with his own feelings in processing something that was never fully explained or shared with him.

While my mother's grief was overwhelming, she never blamed God. It is said that "time heals all wounds," but for parents who lose a child, the hole is always there. I hope I will never have to experience the depth of pain and anguish that my parents went through. My mother passed away at age 96 and Aaron was always in her heart though she seldom talked about him anymore. She still had his picture on the dresser in her assisted-living room. While her grief was so great, she told me that one year after his death, the Lord spoke to her heart. He showed her that she still had two younger children to care for and that it was time to start living again.

Unfortunately, that's not the end of the story. Six months later, my father's business partner died suddenly of a heart attack at age fifty. In the next few years, the other trusted business partner and accountant mishandled the finances and left our family heavily in debt. The American dream had crumbled!

It takes years to gain some understanding of life's tragedies. Only in looking back can we gain perspective of how God is weaving the tapestry of our lives. As a result of the situation, my parents moved to Rapid City, South Dakota, bought land and started over at ages 45 and 55. They refused to declare bankruptcy and began the slow and deliberate process of repaying the debts as well as starting over in business. My mother became the new accountant! She also began the search for a new church! The road of tragedy and grief took an abrupt turn as God began a new chapter in our lives.

A New Life

We loved our new church! Mother knew that she needed to find a church that my younger brother, Steve, and I would love so she wouldn't have to "make" us go to church. She was hungry for more of God, too. She had raised her hand for salvation in our previous church, but never heard from anyone about what it meant. The recent tragedy revealed her raw desire to have an authentic relationship with Christ. Dad wasn't interested yet and let her make the church decision. He attended occasionally at first, and then became more regular as he got acquainted with people. He was impressed that the church had mostly blue-collar, hard-working people just like him. As time passed, he began to feel at home there. Our search for a new church home proved to be practical and rewarding.

Stephen and I made new friends in a new school and new city. We were too young to realize our parents were struggling at a fresh start both in their lives and in their business. My parents bought acreage and began to develop it into a mobile home park. We soon realized that it was "all hands-on deck" as they developed the park, bought trees to plant, built and painted fences, and mowed the newly planted lawns. My father had to quit school in the eighth grade to work in the fields in Sweden to help his mother, so, in his eyes, children were meant for work. And work we did! Some days Mother just told him, "today the kids will play with their friends!" I attribute my strong work ethic to him and am grateful for it, but also know that it can become a crutch for trying to win favor with my heavenly father. I believe that a lot of ministers and their spouses struggle with trying to earn favor with God by working long after others have quit for the day. It becomes a way to curry favor from a heavenly Father they do not really know or understand. They superimpose their understanding of an earthly father's expectations upon their spiritual service and actually lose the joy in their relationship with God.

They filter His involvement through a high-expectation filter that demands much but leaves one depleted and spent.

During my fifth-grade year in elementary school, I chose to accept Christ as my savior. I remember sitting with my mother and brother on the second row in church when I raised my hand. I remember the strange feeling that I must have been bad if someone had to die in my place. I felt guilty and started to think I had to be good to prove I was worthy to love. Children perceive strange things in their innocence and often do not realize the full meaning of God's grace. They still process things through their family metric. I encourage parents reading this book to take seriously the decision of their children to follow Christ and spend the necessary time to help them understand that they do not have to feel guilty in order to receive God's wonderful grace.

As the church family reached out to us as a new family, our social life began to revolve around the activities provided there—class parties, youth events, and family gatherings. Every church has its problems, but Church of the Open Bible in Rapid City, South Dakota, had a good reputation established by a long line of leaders with discernible integrity. They valued adherence to the Bible and discipleship. While in elementary Sunday school, we learned to have devotions, memorize Bible verses, and apply them to our daily lives. The Sunday school "quarterly" or lesson guide offered practical application and accountability to our weekly lessons. We earned points for consistency. It became a natural part of our lives and foundational preparation for our teen years to firmly establish our relationship with Christ. While I look back on that time in my life, I realize how the church provided a set of standards by which to gauge decision-making and life in general. My mother had desired for us to be involved in life on more than just a social setting. She provided the opportunity for us to gain spiritual development and to learn to listen for God's guidance.

Middle School seems to be a traumatic time for most people even though, at the time, we all think we are the only ones with those feelings. I was a good student, but extremely shy! I was a good student because I am intelligent, but I also became physically ill just thinking about having to ask a teacher for help, so I would try to figure out the answers myself. That worked all right except for algebra!

The shyness did not keep me from noticing a cute guy at church. He was two years older and even though I was too introverted to talk to him, his mom was my youth leader. She often had girls' slumber parties at her home, and I used those times to steal a glimpse of him as he came and went from his high school job.

I wonder what it would have been like to be extroverted in those teen years, to have fun and not worry about what other people thought! However, I did *not* want to be noticed. I was content simply to blend into the wallpaper. My self-consciousness made me feel like a misfit! At school, I always looked for others to befriend who also didn't seem to fit in—perhaps out of empathy. During a semester in eighth grade home economics class, we studied personal care and our bodies. At the end, I was voted by the class to have the perfect body size and proportions! The attention from that was very uncomfortable and, in the end, it backfired! I immediately gained fifteen pounds and began a struggle with weight into my early adult years. I'm sure the class's intention was for encouragement, yet it seemed to put more pressure on me to be perfect and I became even more self-conscious.

The seeds of perfectionism—planted by a

myriad of issues, were well on their way to sprouting. While my parents were wonderful parents and did everything to ensure a safe home and food on the table, their personal struggles became a subtle template for how I began to view things and what my reaction and expectations were of others, including my own family. As a parent of three grown and married sons, I know that parents do their best with what they know and mine certainly did their best to provide and love their family. Yet, I also needed to be aware of the factors that motivated me to please and perform perfectly. I knew what I expected, but always ended up shrinking back from the conflict it produced. It was like the proverbial "no man's land" wherein winners were rare, and I needed to gain a sense of adequacy—both in myself and in the lives of my family.

Randy Frost, in his article, "Pitfalls to Perfectionism," in Psychology Today, suggests that we tend to over-concern ourselves with the ramifications and implications of our mistakes and fear they will flavor how others see us and validate our input into their lives. He further suggests that we become haunted by the uncertainty of how our effort was perceived by others and eventually produces obsessive-compulsive tendencies that become, in our way of evaluating others, and ourselves.

Concern with mistakes is a reflection of what Frost calls the core issue in perfectionism, the unspoken belief or doubt that arises in a child's mind that tells them they are incompetent or unworthy. He asserts, "It leads to hyper-criticalness and the rigid adherence to strict standards of performance under all conditions. It is the element of perfectionism most linked to psychopathology. And it comes about because a child has been made to feel that approval is contingent on performance."

While school and social settings produced my greatest feelings of anxiety and social awkwardness, I felt more comfortable in the church setting. I fit in and felt loved and encouraged to grow, with standards of excellence but not pressure to perform. In fact, when I felt a definite call to ministry as a teen, I had no doubt and was surprised that I was able to be firm with my mother that I wanted to go to Bible college. She had always hoped that I would attend a women's college with ties to a social and educational sorority she had long supported. Since she didn't have a college education, I knew that she wanted the best for me, yet she was aware of how God had worked in our family as we transitioned from being a socially connected family before my brother's death to a God-connected family in our new city and church.

The church youth group provided an environment of fun, as well as spiritual growth and I loved my friends there! The cute guy to whom I referred became a good friend! We started group dating when I was fourteen and he was sixteen. He had to gain the permission of the pastor who had to vouch for his character. Then, after being vetted by the pastor, had to gain permission from my mother to drive me home from church. After all, I was only fourteen! Besides being handsome and a high school athletic jock, he had a great sense of humor. Did I mention that our family was very serious? Yes, very serious! Even though I could barely talk to him for two years, he continued to pursue me and it became his challenge to elicit conversation and smiles. When I reached high school, he was still interested in me and I in him. Most people date several other people before finding the right match for life. However, this friendship would later facilitate the merging of two blue-collar, Christian families.

There Had Better Be a Corner!

Chapter 2

The Story Behind the Story – Part 2

"Our determination to learn how to work together as a team paved the way for us to both enjoy the neutral zone of a marriage in which we could mutually encourage and admonish each other in love."

I mentioned earlier that my family was very serious and had a strong work ethic. No time for dreams or play. No time for allowing creative thoughts and activities to influence my development as a "productive member of society." My father's mantra often included justifying our existence by what we produced. That was where a person's true value could be discerned—in what they produced and in how much money they made along the way. Then I married a dreamer and our worlds collided! I was drawn to him because he had a way of enjoying life and being fun to be around. I found myself measuring him against the work ethic modeled by my father. Even though he also had a strong work ethic, my work ethic was off the charts.

When he began to verbalize his dreams, I felt it my duty to keep one of his feet firmly nailed to the ground. After all, someone had to keep this dreamer from disappearing into the clouds. My family never spoke of things we could not quantify, and for him to do so simply seemed unnatural and unhealthy. On the scale of introvert/extroverts, we were complete opposites. He loved highlighting his spontaneous sense of humor. However, I just wanted to blend into the wallpaper and did not want the attention a sense of humor could bring. There were more important things to which we should give our attention and he always talked about how things were "going to get better" just did not compute in my analytical mind. I felt he was out of balance and held an unrealistic assessment of our true financial situation as we struggled to make ends meet in the ministry. I did not understand it at the time, but God had given him his sense of humor as a way to live positively and to be able to inject levity in a heavy situation. My husband drew energy from being around people and interacting with them. We were total opposites at that time and did not understand the dynamics of how marriage relationships develop through working together—not against each other.

Almost five decades later, we have both worked our way to the middle of the chart. He gained a stronger sense of what really motivated me, and I actually began to enjoy the ability to insert a light word or two into a situation fraught with anxiety or fear. Our determination to learn how to work together as a team paved the way for us to both enjoy the neutral zone of a marriage in which we could mutually encourage and admonish each other in love.

As youth pastors, we worked secular jobs during the week and ministry at night and on weekends. Our first ministry salary was a whopping $25 a month. It took me a long time to accept the fact that I was married to a minister and that it was a choice I had willingly made. It just hadn't seemed like it would be so difficult at the time. While I was still very shy and didn't want to speak in front of people, I loved to be on the worship team and sometimes sing with a duet or trio. A pivotal moment came when the pastor's wife asked me to speak at the Mother's Day Luncheon. She said there would be many ladies in attendance that did not always come to the church and they needed to hear a positive message from the church. I remember thinking, "What? I'm not a mother and I'm not a leader!" She reminded me that I was a daughter with a mother and, as a pastor's wife, I was a leader whether I liked it or not. What a revelation! I gulped, ran to my husband, and desperately put together a speech. With knees knocking and a voice barely discernable, I began to speak to them—hoping time would elapse quickly enough to reach the end of this terrible ordeal. I did not want to waste their time and I was sure they did not want it wasted by a novice. I was relieved when they did not throw their centerpieces at me.

A year later, we received a call to pastor a small, struggling church in Wyoming. I was born in Wyoming but had not been back since I was in grade school. The district superintendent painted our recruitment with broad strokes of guilt highlighted by naïve duty. If we didn't come, the church would be forced to close! Our hapless response to his distress call found us moving west and wondering whether or not we did the right thing. We had accepted the call, sight unseen.

After seeing the "church," presently meeting on Main Street in a Roto-Rooter building, we went inside the circa 40's building and saw a makeshift sanctuary. Its decor was non-existent. The walls screamed for a picture or two and the theater-style seats were worn and wobbly. We stood in the midst of our new "parish" and fought back tears. Unable to form an encouraging word, my husband suggested we go across the street to a local eatery and try to eat something. It was one of those dated fried chicken places with a giant rooster above the sign. Finding a place to sit, we ordered and waited for our meal. We just sat there staring at the table unable to form a coherent sentence—which was surprising given Jim's ability to talk about anything, anywhere. He was speechless. What had we done? Was it too late to rescind our acceptance? I waited for his "things will get better" line but it didn't come. Bereft of encouragement he just sat across the table unable to look me in the eye. The fidgeting of his fingers told me he was finally unable to point out the silver lining in our latest adventure. When I saw that, my floundering sense of optimism went underwater.

Unable to eat our greasy meal, we returned to the "church" and discovered our upstairs apartment to be rat-infested and nearly uninhabitable. We moved our things into the apartment and prepared for our first Sunday morning service. The former pastor came by to see us. His first words were, "So . . . do you still feel called to this church?" He chuckled and introduced himself as he stuck out his hand to greet us. We had a sense that he was relieved to no longer be the pastor.

Our first Sunday boasted fifteen people. It

was immediately obvious that we had become the solution to the district superintendent's problem. After securing secular jobs, we moved into a smaller, newer apartment on the other end of town. We knew we could not stay in the Roto-Rooter building if we wanted the congregation to grow. My husband, the "optimist," began scouting for a more appealing place in which to move our congregation. The immediate move found us in a Seventh Day Adventist building near our apartment. The rent was low, and the building was everything a small congregation needed.

After a year, the "optimist" discovered an unfinished, 3000 square foot home. Due to health reasons, the owner could not finish the home and listed the property at a quarter of its value. The property seemed right for a church and boasted a completely finished lower level apartment for us. In order to purchase the property, we needed to obtain a loan from the local bank. After my husband raised enough for a down payment, he took his proposal to the bank. The first one laughed at him. Undaunted, he sought out another—this time with success. Remember, he's a dreamer, nothing is impossible! And, of course, with God, nothing is impossible! I, on the other hand, am a realist and sometimes felt swept away in the current of his dreams. At least for now, things were beginning to look up. We started a day care center on the main level to help pay for the building. Even with the new source of revenue, we decided not to take a salary but instead pay the workers necessary for its successful operation. Living in a basement with no church salary and no viable prospect on the horizon. We managed to eat and pay bills with money from our part-time jobs.

After three years we decided to start a family. We had seen other couples make the same statement and shortly afterward enter into the parenthood category. However, after a year we still had not conceived. Every time I looked at a baby I would cry and yearn to hold my own child in my arms! Just that short time of waiting gave me a tiny glimpse of what infertility must feel like: the tears and the fears wrapped in the immense desire for your own child.

Soon our first son, Kyle, was born in 1975. We attended natural childbirth classes together and Jim was the first trained husband allowed in the delivery room in that Wyoming county! Previous opportunities for husbands in the delivery room had met with untrained distraction. Now, however, husbands trained in the natural childbirth process were welcomed. Kyle was a week late and we were so excited to finally welcome him! After a twelve-hour labor, he checked in at a healthy eight pounds on a cold, stormy, winter evening. Jim and I both noticed a concern sweep the room as the afterbirth did not separate and expel itself. The doctors tactfully declared a state of emergency and asked Jim to leave the room. Jim had functioned according to the training he received, but now the situation demanded his absence. After half an hour, the doctors determined that there were complications with the delivery.

Jim left the delivery room and sat in the hallway waiting and watching the nurses rush past him with pints of blood for me. Knowing he is a detail person; I can only imagine what he must have thought as he watched the frantic activity centering around our son's delivery. He made a long-distance call asking our parents for prayer. Our mothers were frantic and even devised a plan to drive through the blizzard for two hundred miles to help out. Jim assured them that their travel would produce more worry if they ventured out in the blizzard, so instead, they prayed. Eventually, the doctor relayed to him that I had lost a lot of blood and advised him to go home to sleep. How could he sleep? My life was on the line! After several hours he traveled the short distance to our home and had a pivotal encounter with God that night. I was unconscious at the time, so I'll let him describe what happened.

"As I drove home from the hospital, I tried desperately to sort out feelings of happiness mixed with feelings of fear that my wife might not live through the night. I had one of those theological discussions with God. I was still too young to know what God allows and what can be prevented by faith. The day for which we had long waited had quickly become a nightmare. While at the hospital, I had difficulty looking at my son—even though he was unaware of all the commotion. A thousand thoughts fought for recognition as I pulled into my driveway like a zombie. I made my way to the downstairs apartment and found the presence of mind to call a pastor who had been my wife's pastor when she was a little girl. He was a kind, gentle man who had a love for people and had become a friend of the family. He visited with me for a short time then said, "Just remember, it's not what happens to you in life but what you allow it to do to you that matters."

After he left, I stood in front of the fireplace and cried. How could God allow this to happen? I did His work and took little or no pay for it. My sacrifice should amount to something, right? Yet, I could feel His discernable touch on my heart. Soon,

I opened my eyes and said to Him, 'No matter what happens to her, I will serve you with all my heart.' That moment in time became the watershed moment in my life in which I learned I really had no other option than to trust God. Within five minutes, the hospital called and told me that she had regained consciousness and that she was stable. God came through! He did care. To this day, we know that what we commit to Him, He will protect. That incident became the point at which we *knew* we could trust God." – *Jim Beaird*

Fast forward. Remember the lower level apartment with the day care on the main floor? By this time, I'm a tired mom with a cranky newborn baby not sleeping at night and not able to sleep during the day with thirty sets of children's feet directly above. The thin carpet overhead did not mute their running and jumping. My stress mounted. While the daycare business covered the costs of the building, I was not working now, and the financial stress became overwhelming. Remember, I'm the practical one with less exuberant faith to believe for God's provision. Little by little, God did provide, but depression was beginning to exert a grip on me like a giant snake coiled around me intent on squeezing out what life I had left. I kept asking God, "if we are called to do your work, aren't you supposed to help a little?" I don't recall whether or not I actually expected an answer, but by then, it didn't matter.

I read about depression and how those gripped in its clutches survive. The pattern seemed to fit me to a tee. I recognized it as an, endless, spiraling descent into a dark, unknown abyss. A sense of powerlessness overwhelms without providing any handle to stop the fall. It thrusts the mind into a circular loop of paralyzing fear and thoughts of further failure. I remember tormenting myself with questions like, "Why is my baby crying? He's not hungry or wet. What am I doing wrong? I'm a terrible mom!" These are all typical emotions for a new mom, but the enemy of our soul skillfully exploits them to infect the heart with poisonous lies—lies that cloud perspective and deflate self-worth. That was me! Deflated, angry, and feeling worthless. I felt our calling into ministry only exacerbated feelings that most women feel at one time or another. I kept wondering if there was another way to navigate through the minefield of motherhood and ministry.

After three years in Wyoming, the church grew from fifteen to fifteen! It wasn't the same fifteen people though, as some died, and a new

young family started attending and had received
Christ. It fueled our faith to see them grow!
However, I did question God about the growth and
asked, "What is the point of us being here three
years without much growth in the church? Are we
failures?" His reply was, "I'm growing you and Jim! I
want you to learn to be faithful in all circumstances."
I have since learned that a pastor's first church is
more about growing him for the ministry than
church numerical growth. As we look back, we both
agree that while there could have been an easier way
to gain ministry skill, nothing could have prepared us
to trust God like time in our first pastorate did. We
don't like to admit to needing character formation or
spiritual growth, but that was God's plan—growing
us.

During the three years in Wyoming, we often
retreated to visit our district director's church of
about three hundred in Colorado Springs. We loved
the worship and fresh life of the Holy Spirit evident
there and soon he asked us to join the staff. We were
thrilled to be in a larger church with a supportive
staff, with young families, and to live in beautiful,
sunny Colorado! Sheridan, Wyoming, was beautiful
in the spring and summer, but very cold in the
winter! Our second son, Jeffrey, was born in
Colorado Springs five weeks late at a healthy nine

pounds! Having been briefed on my previous birthing complications, the doctors were well prepared for any abnormality. I remember our relief when the whole birth process went perfectly and God seemed to be saying, "See, I told you that what you commit to me I will protect. I have plans for you. Just be patient." A third son, Nate, was later born perfectly and also in great health. All three sons have excelled in life and have married wonderful women of God. Yes . . . God IS faithful!

Chapter 3

The Black Hole and the Giant Snake

"Breaking the habit of negative thinking requires a conscious process to replace it with an expression of gratefulness. Gratefulness generates a perspective whose focus is on a heavenly Father who only wants us to know we can trust Him."

I feel it is important to share with you my qualifications for dealing with the topic, "Dreams of the Heart." If you are a dreamer or visionary, you may not think it necessary. However, if not, to dream seems overwhelming and elusive! I definitely did not consider myself a dreamer, which is why it is such a miracle of God's transforming work in my life that I have found my place in that arena.

It is common for dating couples to be attracted to their opposite personality type. As I mentioned in a previous chapter, my husband, Jim, is a visionary and dreamer. I am a realist and want a plan for everything! It was a frustration to me until I understood the positives and negatives and how we balance each other. We dated through high school and college and were married in 1971. Since then, we have learned to navigate our differences into a balance that empowers us both. We no longer look at each other like opposites. We realize that life's process and God's plan for our lives have gradually and purposefully molded us together—without losing individual identities but enjoying each other's strengths and balancing each other's weaknesses.

My husband and I co-pastored for thirty years in Minnesota, Wyoming, Colorado, and Iowa. In 1979, we started a new church in Castle Rock, Colorado with a group of thirty people. We were young and it seemed exciting to try to carve "something out of nothing." It wasn't long before we had too much on our plate—planting a new church, building our home, raising three young sons, and working other jobs to support the church and ourselves.

I had wrestled with depression and sleeplessness since my teen years, but now it seemed that I could no longer suppress it. I was unaware of the signs of depression and my church background did not encourage acknowledgment of it. In fact, any discussion of depression was discouraged. The teaching was that if we loved God, read the Bible, and prayed, nothing else was needed. We were told by older ministers to not talk about weaknesses.

People would not accept our leadership if we did.

After our third son was born, the burden of all my responsibilities overwhelmed me and I decided to seek help. I discovered I suffered from a combination of hormonal and circumstantial depression. It involved food and esteem issues. I discovered that I was not alone in struggling with depression. Whenever I talk about it to women, there is a sense of relief that this ugly secret can be breached and discussed. On several occasions, I've ministered in retreats and conferences to women struggling with this issue. Watching the light come on in their eyes makes my own previous struggles with depression worthwhile. It is life-giving to share life after depression. To this day, I believe that a great many ministry couples toil under a false sense of perception. They were taught that if they showed a weakness, people would not respect or follow them. Transparency was considered a deal breaker for effective ministry. After all, how can one lead if they admit to weakness or struggle? I have since learned that the honesty of my own transparency provided a lifeline to those caught in the swirling sea of depression and who felt there would never be a way out.

I describe depression as a black hole! Once

the slide down into the abyss of darkness begins, it seems impossible to escape! My husband enjoys science fiction and has on more than one occasion watched as a spaceship was sucked helplessly into an interstellar black hole—never to be heard from again. For him, it was science fiction. For me, it was *non*-fiction. I felt helpless as I neared the black hole of depression. I also describe it as a giant snake that squeezes the life right out of a person. The snake crushes its victim's ribs so it cannot breathe. Eventually, the prey succumbs to the snake's tightening death grip and the next step is for the snake to swallow the dead victim. Either way, the enveloping depression was ominous and ever-present.

Another fact about depression is that many go through it thinking it is just a normal part of life and that either it will subside or remain until the black hole or giant snake finishes its work. If it subsides, great. If it doesn't, what is the use of trying to do something purposeful with one's life? I must point out here that many think suicide is the only escape hatch available in the spaceship heading toward the black hole. Those statistics are both frightening and sobering. Having seen the black hole *and* the giant snake, I have hope for you. God's purpose for you is to live a full life and no less!

So, how did I escape the black hole and the giant snake? At the recommendation of a friend who had been on a similar journey, I eventually sought counseling from a Christian psychologist. The idea of seeking help from a counselor was something considered taboo by the clergymen we had looked up to and was perceived as a sign of weakness. I was ready to get past the past and forge ahead into a new and different future—hopefully, one that held health and wholeness as its standard and gave me permission to develop any gifts God had deposited into my life as a sacred trust. As I first met with her, she encouraged me to begin a journal describing my feelings and when they began. Over the next few years, the internal struggle of the lies I had believed was exposed. The light of God's word replaced them and I gradually experienced reprieve from the black hole of depression and the death grip of the giant snake. The most wonderful thing I experienced during this time was finding out that I controlled what happened to me. I felt the snake's death grip loosening until it no longer had me in its grasp and the shallow gasps of breathing turned into great gulps of life and freedom. I had God's help through a valuable resource that He had prepared in advance because He knew what the enemy had in store for my life. I gained perspective about the whole map of life instead of remaining stuck in one of life's little detours. I was able to discover my unique design as both a woman and a woman called of God.

Was that a one-time fix for life? No. I discovered that maintaining freedom from depression is a personal maintenance program and that I needed to be ever mindful of its subtle tactics. Several years ago, I felt a tinge of depression or darkness coming into my day. At that moment, I decided it was too much work to dig out of the black hole and that I had the choice right then to stop it. "I don't have the energy to go there anymore!" I said. I felt empowered to take control and set boundaries on feelings of self-pity by replacing them with intentional expressions of gratitude. Breaking the habit of negative thinking requires a conscious process to replace it with an expression of gratefulness. Gratefulness generates a perspective whose focus is on a heavenly Father who only wants us to know we can trust Him. He wrote a wonderful plan for our lives and to realize that we have not slipped out of his loving care seals the deal. It actually becomes our mindset instead of always wondering if He forgot us or left our development on autopilot. We enter into a state of continual God-consciousness because we learn that not only is He ever-present, He is also ever active in our lives.

It's amazing how gratitude changes our focus from what we don't have to all the wonderful things we enjoy – relationships, friends, family, and material possessions. Paul states a simple truth in I Timothy 6:6, "Godliness with contentment is great gain." Gratefulness is a state of contentment in which we reflect on how full our life is instead of comparing it to what other people have. During extended times alone together or during travel, my husband and I regularly expound on God's goodness and blessings. It is hard to let resentment into our hearts when we consciously fill them with the attitude of gratitude. Currently, I do not remember a time when traveling across Tampa Bay on the causeway bridge that one of us did not say, "Thank you Father for allowing us to live in Tampa." Our perspective on life now centers on the faithfulness of His providence—both in what He brought us through and in where He desires to take us.

Lay the backpack down!

I don't think we realize how much energy gets drained from us when we obsess and worry about burdens and cares. As a mom, I thought it was necessary for me to always be thinking and worrying about something. I remember the day when I made a conscious decision to disconnect myself from the pull of incessant worry. Once again, it had been at work again in a subtle, yet deliberate way to pull me back to the black hole with all the other worries I had felt before. This time my normal aging process was the catalyst to get my attention shifted from trusting God to the dread of getting older.

Our oldest son had graduated from high school. I felt a sense of relief in that milestone for one of our children. My fortieth birthday loomed on the horizon—just two years away! I remember attending birthday parties for others who turned forty and I felt that, even though the parties were meant to be fun, I looked at them as funeral preparatory exercises. I determined mine would be different. The others had black balloons, black roses, and tombstones. The gifts were comprised of products for senior citizens. The whole idea repulsed me! I cannot understand why I had such a visceral reaction to celebrating an age that everyone else told me, "That's where life begins—at your fortieth birthday!" I didn't see it as the beginning of anything positive. Yet, I felt the weight of it upon my spirit and once again began to fight the old thoughts beckoning to me from my redeemed past. I even wondered if the giant snake had babies who grew up and came after me.

I determined to be ready physically, mentally, and spiritually for my fortieth birthday. I had struggled for years with weight issues and losing the proverbial ten pounds. I resumed a physical exercise program, which not only helped physically, but also gave mental clarity and optimism.

As the date approached for my fortieth birthday, I dropped not-too-subtle hints to my husband that I did not want a traditional black-decorated occasion to commemorate this milestone in my life! I was not about to allow myself to fit into the stereotype of those who jokingly accepted the aging process as if they had no choice. I still could not identify the source of my feelings of negativity toward this particular day, but I think my husband got the message. He knew from the tone in my voice that something was emerging from deep within my heart. I was going to break the mold and emancipate all those women who, like me, felt helplessly destined to grow old without significance or purpose—kind of a Joan of Arc of the middle-aged set. The very thought of asserting myself ran counter to my personality. But something had changed as a glimmer of hope began to sparkle in the recesses of the dark depression I had felt for so long.

I began to sense that I had willingly sold out to a life wherein dreams were forbidden, and the diligence of busyness was all that really mattered. Evidently, I had become compliant with the covert process of surrendering hopes, dreams and aspirations to the treadmill of thankless duty. I was turning forty, but, as they say, life would for me, BEGIN at forty and I would escape the diabolical snare associated with keeping both feet on the ground. Maybe my husband was right. Maybe God allows us to have dreams that point to a more fulfilling life and which point to possibilities through developing gifts he's given me. Maybe not. I had never considered the backpack of responsibility to actually be a metaphorical anchor keeping me stuck in one place, nurturing a destructive mindset, and allowing me to only turn circles around a fixed point—the point of expectations by others.

Then, in one of those quiet times when God had my attention and the cares and concerns of my life seemed distant, I felt like God was asking me a question. "Are you ready to lay down the backpack, Kris?" I didn't even have to ask what he meant. He'd been watching me struggle with my distorted perception both of his love and my belabored response to it. He'd seen my futile attempts to please him and fill the role of the practical one in a marriage—you know, the one who sacrifices challenge and opportunity for safety and security. The backpack was stuffed with unrealistic expectations—both of others and me. I know there were times when my husband felt he couldn't win no matter what he said to me or what he did to try to bring perspective into my myopic outlook on life. It had grown so full that its weight kept me close to the ground and suffocated my own hopes and desires. God wanted to change the way I perceived Him and get rid of the things that prevented me from feeling the intimacy of His love in my heart. I began to realize that I had done a good job of insulating and isolating my heart until it was literally impervious to His touch. Wow. I had only allowed Him into my life when He could fit through the metric of my ability to receive what He had for me. Again, it was on my terms, not His.

I began to realize that I had been carrying around a bag of seeds—those from which depression grew and those from which additional responsibilities kept me from standing upright. "What-if" seeds provided much of the additional weight: what if my child gets hurt, what if there isn't enough money for this or that, or what if I'm not good enough. God's question was divinely timed. It provided a sense of relief that I could trust him with

the weight I'd accumulated in my backpack. Maybe
the vanity of responsibility was its own demon. The
decision was not difficult. Immediately, I said, "Yes,
God, I would love to lay it down!" It was at that
moment that I realized even though He gave me
victory over the pull of the black hole and the grip of
the giant snake, I had placed those things in my
backpack just in case I might need them later. It was
then that I realized I had not allowed Him to *destroy*
the things that threatened me. My backpack had a
zipper and I could easily access my old demons.

A few days before my birthday, Jim threw a
surprise party for me and it really did surprise me!
Amazingly, there was none of the black
paraphernalia attached to a fortieth party and no
senior citizen gifts, just very nice gifts. On the way to
work that day, I heard the announcement, "Happy
birthday to Kris Beaird who is forty, fit, and foxy!"
Wow – Jim did it and with creativity, too! When I
walked into my office area, a co-worker asked if it
was my birthday. He heard the announcement on
the radio but couldn't believe it was me they were
talking about. I smiled and nodded! It felt good to be
taking control of my life in a positive way and realize
that others were rejoicing with me. As the fortieth
came and went, I realized that I'd laid down the
backpack of self-centeredness and exchanged it for a

garment of gratefulness. I chose to never look back. I chose life over lingering death. I chose to be the new creation He redeemed me to be. I chose to cast my fears in the sea of God's forgetfulness and never trust a zippered bag again.

Part 2: Lessons from Around the "Corner"

The journey to the "corner" to which I keep referring is meant to be a message of hope to anyone who has ever felt they must just endure their time on earth and go through the motions of mediocrity and disillusionment. I feel that one of the greatest disappointments of all is telling oneself that there is nothing more than their present lot in life. When I once said, "There had *better* be a corner!" my perspective was limited to what I felt at the time. Since then, I see a much bigger picture of all the possibilities that come as blessings once I got past the corner. The journey simply strengthened and prepared me for what was beyond that point.

There Had Better Be a Corner!

Chapter 4

Baggage or Luggage?

"Satan wants our eyes fixed on the rear-view mirror by constantly reminding us where we've been and what we've done."

When a person transitions from one place to another in their personal relationship with God, it is amazing to gain perspective over the things that had earlier tried to derail our lives. I call that, "looking through our God-lens." Some cannot see clearly until they don their eyeglasses. Our spiritual outlook is similarly challenged. Even though we may know the Bible from cover to cover, it isn't until we see things from God's perspective that we gain a clear perspective of our very existence.

Let me share what I consider to be a major point of application in gaining proper perspective for what you might be doing right now. God is not in a hurry with our development nor is He deficient in patience. The things we think we need to hang onto are usually things that prevent strategic advancement in our spiritual development. I call those things "baggage." Yes, we are quite skilled at collecting all sorts of baggage—thinking that they are things that are actually a part of us and how we were made to function. Just as the artist needs to step back and gain overall perspective, we need to step back and determine if baggage has taken the place of our luggage. Baggage. Luggage. What's the difference? Perspective. Let me illustrate by sharing from another angle.

When an artist paints a scene, he or she often steps back to look at it to see if they are creating the right lighting, texture, and mood. They check for accuracy of detail and clarity of thematic elements painted into the impression they are trying to create. Older artists know by experience just what needs to be added or painted over. They understand that every painting needs foundational elements upon which they can create a meaningful and lasting impression. The novice simply doesn't know what needs to be in the basic foundation for each picture. That makes them no less an artist. As they stick with it and determine to learn how to convey what's in their mind to what ends up on canvas, their work improves and eventually becomes an expression of their original intent. They sometimes learn that less is more and that too many details can delay the finished product. A proper perspective enables them to rightly convey the image or message they endeavor to replicate on canvas for all to see and understand.

While I do not consider myself an artist, I can appreciate good art when I see it. I can tell when the artist was in a hurry or whether or not he or she was even any good to begin with. I have seen art that looked hurried labeled as abstract art and found myself thinking, "Gee, even I could have painted that." The truth of the matter is that we all tend to just do enough to get by and still call ourselves productive individuals. The quality of our life's application falls into the abstract category with no clear definition of what might be in the Father's heart. Proper perspective became the victim to hurried and harried planning and the result was anything but aesthetic or useful.

My husband and I enjoy traveling—either to see family and friends or for business. We have our system for packing and making sure we do not forget essentials for the trip. In the English language, the words baggage and luggage are synonymous. However, for the sake of illustration, let me draw upon modern word pictures associated with each word. Luggage is generally associated with the suitcases we pack for a trip and contains the essentials for a successful venture. "Luggage" conveys the idea of careful planning with just the right choice of clothing to suit the occasion. If one is vacationing, their suitcase might include sandals, shorts, and casual wear. If the reason for the trip is business, then more formal attire is necessary.

If a person tends to always be drawn into interpersonal battles either with self or others, they are said to have a lot of "baggage." I heard a couple ladies talking one day and one said to the other, "Have you ever noticed so-and-so?" The other replied, "I'd never go out with him. He has a lot of baggage." She meant that he had more problems than she was willing to deal with in the potential relationship. I define **baggage** as heavy weights that hold us back from the fulfillment of our purpose and passion. Hebrews 12:1 tells us to **"throw off everything that hinders and the sin that so easily entangles** and let us run with perseverance the race marked out for us."

The determination to identify baggage in our lives prompts us to step back and see just what we have been carrying in our backpack or baggage. It may seem obvious, but the first weight is sin, which is violation of God's laws. Let God search our hearts and reveal anything offensive to Him. We need to understand that the enemy of our soul has an assignment to **steal, kill,** and **destroy** everything God wants for us to live in victory.

- He will **steal** our vision, hopes, dreams and joy by introducing discouragement, defeat, despair and depression.
- He will **kill** our physical body and mental capacity by introducing sickness, disease, mental disorders, and suicidal thoughts.
- He will **destroy** our relationships by introducing confusion, selfishness, betrayal, and destructive choices.

At this point, I just want to ask you to step back and get a perspective of what you have been carrying around in your baggage. Look at it as an artist might step back and look at their painting. What's out of balance? What doesn't belong? Are you having trouble identifying some of the "besetting weights?" Let me help with a few observations of my own. I have shared these with several women's groups around the country as I ministered in their conferences. I am sure you will identify with these observations and, in the end, determine to stop carrying them around. I call them the "big three." Guilt, shame, and condemnation.

Guilt

Guilt is how we feel about **things** in our lives that were wrong or sinful or what we have done in the past. It is a normal and honest response to our conscience. God's solution to guilt is to accept Christ's forgiveness and to release both ourselves and others from the tangled web of deceit from the enemy. However, it can be like last month's newspapers that we don't throw away if we do not release it to others and receive it for ourselves. We keep stacking them in the corner until there are more and more stacks taking over our living space. We actually become a hoarder of things about which we feel or felt guilty. Guilt tells us that we are unworthy of good things and that we probably got what we deserved. Guilt is the enemy's way of robbing us of living in a debris-free spiritual environment. He wants lots of clutter—choking out the things God wants to use to revive our spirit and open our eyes to what's ahead. Satan wants our eyes fixed on the rear-view mirror by constantly reminding us where we've been and what we've done. We cannot step back and gain perspective because we find our self locked in the past. We have accepted the accusations of the enemy and have resigned our self to living out the consequences of our past choices. Sound familiar?

Guilt was one of my "big three." You might ask, "What did you have to feel guilty about?" As I mentioned in a previous chapter, I grew up in a loving home and attended a very healthy church. You might think I would never be a target for the enemy's guilt bombs. Wrong. Even in that healthy and wholesome environment, he found a way to sneak a deadly package of guilt into my young heart. I want to make something clear before I go any further. You do not have to have done something terrible or sinful in order to experience guilt. You only have to agree with the enemy that you will never be enough. He'll tell you, "You could have done that better . . . or differently. It's wrong and it's your fault." Or, "You haven't suffered enough."

I was never an immoral person. I was never a rebellious teenager. I was never even given to crude talk. Part of my guilt stemmed from growing up in a wholesome environment while others did not. That's how the enemy operates. He can take something good in your life and make you feel bad about it. While you may have survived some of the things that others got caught up in, you begin to experience what psychologists call "survivor's guilt." We recently had a mass shooting in a school here in Florida in which 17 high school students and adults were shot to death before police could stop the rampage. More than a year later, two more deaths were attributed to the horrific event. These additional deaths occurred when two individuals committed suicide after struggling with not having been murdered when many of their friends met an untimely death at the hands of a deranged gunman. They had "survivor's guilt." The gunman did not get to them during the shooting, but they still became one of his statistics after the tragic event. Many parents were relieved and grateful to learn their children had not been involved in the shooting. Perhaps nobody was really prepared to deal with such an unimaginable and devastating event that would have many rethinking their whole perspective on school safety. At any rate, just because the shooting ended and the shooter was taken out of the picture, the underlying current of devastation pulled two more victims to their deaths.

Guilt can become the tool the enemy uses on those who have made wrong choices and ended up regretting them the rest of their lives or even for those who lived a sheltered life. He can accuse you both for what you did and for what never happened to you. You can find yourself in the role of the survivor who questions why you survived while others did not. I am reminded of the directorial premier of Robert Redford in 1980 when he directed the acclaimed movie, "Ordinary People" starring Mary Tyler Moore and Donald Sutherland. It was a story about the accidental death of their older son in a boating accident. Moore played the bitter mother, Sutherland played the good-natured father, and Timothy Hutton played the guilt-ridden younger son. The whole story frames the sorrowing family dealing with the tragedy each in their own way. While the mother was very bitter and angry and the father tried to salve things over to maintain family equilibrium, the younger son who survived the incident that took his brother's life found himself fighting the onslaught of guilt at having survived the tragedy. The poignant power of family dynamics during the "coming to grips" with a loss left many in the theaters crying as they identified with similar dynamics in their lives.

I saw this same scenario play out in our family after my older brother's deadly car accident while a student at the university. So much attention was focused on his death that another of my siblings was inadvertently left out of the grieving process until much later. I outlined this family event in a previous chapter, but I felt it necessary to recount it again in illustration of survivor's guilt. The enemy will try to make you feel guilty for the life God gave you and the protection He afforded you while living it.

Shame

Shame is how we feel about **perceptions** in our lives that were inaccurate or misinterpreted. We see ourselves as damaged goods. Shame can also come either from the things we have done or things that have happened to us, such as sexual abuse or violation. There is no greater crippler than shame. Once a person sees themselves as damaged goods, their self-perceived value plummets and the enemy buries health under heaps of accusations. The enemy designs shame to delete our worth and deplete our energy. Shame becomes the metric through which everything else in one's life gets measured. As long as shame exists, mental, physical, and spiritual health remains elusive. Past sin becomes present power preventing an individual from moving on and getting past the past.

Shame tells us that we are not worthy of respect and honor. It often drives us to accept second best in life since we are too full of shame to accept the very best. We simply do not deserve it— at least that's what we tell ourselves. Our self-atonement keeps us from engaging in healthy relationships and extending and receiving trust from those close to us. It keeps us in a self-imposed prison with no view of what we could really become if we would just let God cleanse us from our guilt and allow us to see ourselves as He sees us. The guilt trap becomes a deadly snare. Psalm 25:14 says, "The Lord confides in those who fear him; he makes his covenant known to them. My eyes are ever on the Lord, for only He will release my feet from the snare." He wants to release us from our near-sighted shame perspective and give us the big view of His great love and forgiveness.

I am reminded of the classic historical romance novel, The Scarlet Letter, by Nathaniel Hawthorne in which women taken in adultery were given a red "A" on their foreheads to forever be a symbol of shame for their actions. The novel's main character, Hester, became the unwilling recipient of such designation. While the scarlet letter was meant to be a symbol of shame. It instead it became a powerful symbol of identity to Hester. The letter's meaning shifts as time passes in the romantic story. Originally intended to mark Hester as an adulteress, the "A" eventually comes to stand for "Able." The emphasis shifted from being an accused outcast to becoming a person capable of power and influence. That's the picture of redemption—God's redemption. He has removed the designation of "forever guilty and worthy of shame" to forever victorious and worthy of honor.

Somewhere along the line I became angry
with God. I was disappointed in something about
our relationship and felt only an anger towards Him.
I could not pray or read my Bible during those
weeks and months I struggled for a glimpse of His
approval. Our little church had struggled to be able
to pay us amidst the financial upheaval of the 1980's.
I felt that our own financial struggle must be a
reflection of how He viewed our efforts to grow the
church. Was He mad at us? Did He even care about
all we were trying to do to keep the church together?
I began to feel a great load of guilt and shame. I
didn't know why, but it was there like a giant rock—
right in the middle of my heart.

My struggle with guilt and shame was not
from having lived a shameful life full of shameful
deeds. I recall a time when our sons were young, and
we worked bi-vocationally to support ourselves
while planting a church in beautiful Colorado. On a
particular day, I was doing the laundry. As I carried
some of the folded clothes to our bedroom, I felt
overcome by a sense of shame and unworthiness. I
dropped the basket by the sofa and fell to my knees
as I buried my face in the cushion and sobbed
uncontrollably. Nobody was around and I felt secure
in letting out the pent-up emotions. I could not
explain what was happening—only that tears were

flowing like a dam had burst somewhere. I kept trying to understand my feelings and why I even felt this way.

I recall a sense of not being alone there in the room by the sofa. An overwhelming sense of God's presence enveloped me, and I felt the unmistakable invitation to look into His face. At first, I did nothing but evaluate the feeling before I dismissed it as random and insignificant. Then, it was almost like I heard Him say, "Look into my face." Initially, the only image I had of a father was that of my own. I immediately remembered my father's stern face as he would just give me the "look" when I did something wrong. In those days, parents were allowed to spank their children as a means of punishment or correction. He never spanked me. The "look" was enough! While kneeling by the couch I again heard God's invitation. "Look into my face." I realized that He wanted to change my perception of His love. He said to imagine a picture of Him like the one of His son, Jesus, we had on our refrigerator. As my mind quickly conjured up that image, I saw Him as a loving and gentle man reaching out his hand to me and, instead of a stern, furrowed brow, He had a smile. I felt the inviting gaze of His kind eyes penetrate my misplaced emotions as He seemed to melt the icy image of a stern gaze I had held onto for so long.

After a few moments of enjoying His welcome and transforming presence, He seemed to ask, "What do you think I think of you?" I told Him I felt He must be ashamed of me. He said, "Shame? Why would you feel shame? You're precious to me and I love you so much that I have never left your side." Yet, for some reason, I felt the shame of not being enough of a minister's wife and mother. Immediately, I reached for my Bible and looked up scriptures dealing with shame. I found Psalm 34:4-5. As I read through it, I felt my heart lighten as the words literally jumped off the page and into my over-analytical mind. "I sought the Lord and He heard me and delivered me from all my fears. They looked to Him and were radiant, and their faces were not ashamed." I read the passage over and over like I had just received a letter from an attorney informing me of an unknown inheritance. I had never seen this before, even though I had read the Bible through many times. Yet, the attorney of heaven delivered the best news I could receive. He wanted to remove my shame—even though it was not based in shameful actions from my past. I had allowed the enemy to beguile me and accuse me of things Jesus had already cleansed by His shed blood so many years ago. I realized that if a person does not have a sordid past from which the enemy can draw accusations, he will take the good things and make us feel ashamed of our blessings. That, together with my increasing depression, became a toxic mixture of poisonous self-image and God consciousness.

Condemnation

Together with guilt and shame, **condemnation** is the accusing voice of the enemy telling us we are unworthy and sentences us to a lifetime of mental and spiritual prison. Remember, guilt and shame were the feelings produced by external situations—whether or not we were really in the wrong. In this case, the external force is the enemy of our soul. He is the voice behind both the megaphone *and* the accusing whisper. He tells us we are not worthy of God's love, grace and forgiveness. After all, why would God love someone like us?

The enemy seeks to condemn us because he's already been condemned when Jesus toppled his earthly kingdom and ruined his legal claim on mankind. He knows his days are numbered so he can only rally supporters by giving them untrue pictures of themselves and their lives. Like some of the news media's claim that others produce a "fake news" that diverts the truth and accuses someone else of what they may be guilty of themselves. Who really has the truth? God the Father does. He already defeated the accuser and the only thing keeping his children from living in the victory He provided is their willingness to believe the "fake news" of the enemy.

I'm certain that I did not exhaust the list of "baggage" items we tend to carry around. From a woman's point of view, these are the big three items that seem to weigh the most in their baggage. Most women will identify with the list and could probably add more of their own. Guilt, shame, and condemnation were my heaviest weights. They were my "baggage."

On the other hand, **luggage** contains the items needed for the future. I tease my husband because he's always looking for the consummate piece of luggage. Since we travel a great deal, one of his favorite stores is the luggage store and whatever quality suitcase or travel satchel is on sale. It seems that for him, the ideal trip is the one taken with great suitcases in which the expectations of the trip ahead get minimized by his attention to packing detail. I think he would not have to travel at all as long as he could shop for the right travel accessory. **Luggage gives us optimistic anticipation of an adventure ahead!** Look at this exciting verse from Romans

8:15 in The Living Bible, **"This resurrection life you received from God is not a timid, grave-tending life. It's adventurously expectant, greeting God with a childlike, 'What's next, Papa?'"**

As believers and disciples, we are given the privilege to develop our lives to influence others positively. If we are content to stay in one place, future promise gets sacrificed on the altar of present provision. Contentment with our near-sighted perspective often robs us of the "hungry eyes" needed for pushing on to the next level of development in our lives. But we are destined to be WOMEN OF INFLUENCE both now and for the next generation! They are crying for mentors to step up to the plate and lead them. **Pack for the future! Get rid of your "baggage"** and start packing for an adventure. You may say, "But I am not a leader!" You may not have a position of leadership, **but** you are **responsible** to develop the gifts and abilities **that God has given you** personally. It is not the responsibility of anyone else – your parents, spouse, friends, or co-workers. It belongs to you. My husband always teaches, "It was God who called you. Only He can do that. It's your responsibility to be a good **steward** of that call."

If we are to be people of influence, there are (at least) four components of the leadership qualities God is developing in us right now. It is time to pack our luggage with the right outfits.

L – Life-Long Learner:

II Timothy 2:15 urges us to "study to show yourself approved; a workman who does not need to be ashamed." Within three years, most information is out-of-date. Yet, we hold onto the things with which we are most comfortable and familiar. While God's principles and message do not change, **our methods of reaching this generation must** change if we are to be the effective leaders we were called to be.

- **Lead**: yourself, your family, your sphere of influence, the next generation...
- **Prayer**: "Lord, help me to grow in You." Leading helps ME to grow! (like having kids helps parents to grow up!) Don't Quit: marriages, kids, church. DON'T QUIT!

E – EQUIP yourself.

God has entrusted you with gifts and abilities.

Find out what they are and develop them. Make yourself accountable to a mentor or teacher who will push you past your level of comfort. Expand your comfort zone with new people, new experiences, and new goals. Accept it willingly with prompt obedience. Do you realize that you can insult God by discounting or ignoring His gifts? Paul said to Timothy: "Stir up the gift that is within you!"

Stirring up the gift in us requires work. It is not simply something we come to a mental assent about. God had placed gifts of communication and leadership within me, but I had not developed them. God opened a unique door for me to earn my master's degree and become certified as a leadership coach through John Maxwell's leadership organization. Countless doors opened that had been previously closed.

A – ACTION

Be willing to step up and be a person of positive influence for the present leadership in your home, church, or community. Be **pro-active.** After decades of working in the church with my husband and in the regional office for our denomination, I felt God challenging me to get out of the church and into the community. At first, I feared that doing so would drain me of anything I had left and that, since

I didn't know anyone "out there," my time would be useless and fruitless. As I emerged from the safety of my religious cocoon, I was met with favor and welcome. People seemed drawn to what I do and the services I can provide the professional community. I began meeting with business staffs to train them in how to work together efficiently and productively. One thing led to another. God called and prompted me, and I responded without realizing I had much to offer our community. I now live in the daily expectation of momentum that only comes from Him in response to my obedience.

Do you realize that our relationship dynamics change with people when we are growing? Some will grow with us, but we'll need to let go of the low energy level maintained by others. Their unwillingness to grow consigns them to a future that only resembles the template of their past.

D – DREAM BIG!

God has **already** placed a dream within our hearts – it resides in our desires and hopes. We need to discover it, write it down, and develop a plan for its implementation. He is waiting with excitement for us to see it fulfilled! I remember listening to others speak of their dreams. I also remember my visceral silence in response to such frivolous thinking. The only thing that had ever come from my response was a kind of jealousy in my heart toward those who could justify dreaming.

While taking a ReFocus® (Terry Walling) class with my husband, one part of the class dealt with giving oneself permission to dream and then to own their dreams. Of course, you know already what I'm going to say. I thought, "How could this frivolous exercise be of any benefit to me? I'm the practical one and that's the way it is going to be. There." Then, when God's still small voice just wouldn't leave me alone, I heard Him say, "Kris, what are your dreams?" I wanted to scream, but instead I said, "Fine. So, you want me to dream. Ok, here are three dreams I have had for some time. One, I want to work together with my husband full time in ministry. Two, I want to work with women in a more meaningful way. And, three, I want to travel to places in this country and around the world I have never seen. There. Satisfied?"

God must have a sense of humor. He'd have to have one in order to process my misinterpretation of His blessings. (I filed those seminar notes away and did not look at them again for two years.) Shortly after revealing to Him my dreams, He called us to leave our positions in Iowa and move to

Florida to become overseers of a region including seven states, 40 churches, and about 100 ministers. I happened to look at my notes from the ReFocus seminar with my list of three dreams I desired to see come into reality someday. I realized that God was in the process of bringing those dreams into fruition. I was working full-time with my husband and traveling to places I had never before visited and cultures I had never experienced.

A few years later I was elected to be the national director for women's ministry within our movement—a capacity in which I served for ten years. When not working with women, I traveled with my husband to all five geographical regions of the United States and about ten countries. As I look back on my reaction to His question about my dream, I now realize that He had been waiting for me to shift gears and get my ears and eyes open to hear and see what He wanted to accomplish through my dreams. "What's next, Papa?"

Chapter 5

Defining Moments: "Write Your Story"

"There are times in our lives when everything takes a turn and things once experienced never again resurface. It's like turning onto a superhighway from a dirt road. We go from making slow progress on a bumpy road to really making progress on a smooth and well-maintained thoroughfare."

The journey to the "corner" to which I keep referring is meant to be a message of hope to anyone who has ever felt they must just endure their time on earth and go through the motions of mediocrity and disillusionment. I feel that one of the greatest disappointments of all is telling oneself that there is nothing more than their present lot in life. When I once said, "There had *better* be a corner!" my perspective was limited to what I felt at the time. Since then, I see a much bigger picture of all the possibilities that come as blessings once you get past the corner. The journey simply strengthens and prepares you for what is beyond that point.

I love the story of Ruth. The four chapters of the book of Ruth tell her story. She married a foreign man whose family fled their country because of famine. We don't even know if she loved him. Then he dies, his brother and father die, and the wives are left alone. Ruth's only point of contact was her mother-in-law, Naomi. She did not know what to do since she was a foreigner with no status and without a husband. Her eyes were fixed on her mother-in-law in hopes she could gain both protection and insight as to how to deal with this major setback in her life. Understand that all three women found themselves in the same, exact situation—the loss of a spouse. Theirs was a culture wherein the men gave status to the women by becoming their property—even if it was to become their spouse. So, it appears that the only way they could have protection and security was to find a man who would marry them. Even then, they had no guarantees that the man would treat them kindly or with affection. The dilemma begins. Three women alone in a foreign land with an uncertain future who were about to write their own stories in an uncertain setting.

I think mothers-in-law get a bad rap. Naomi is one who, in all of her weakness, was an example to Ruth. She became depressed and hopeless, but Ruth still saw an inner strength in her. I met my mother-in-law when I was eleven years old as I walked into her Sunday School class, then later in youth group. I eventually married her son! Now, in her mid-nineties, she still lives close to us in Brandon. She is not only my mother-in-law but also a dear friend I can always depend on for her prayers and love. Ruth lost her husband, but Naomi lost her husband and two sons in a foreign land! I cannot fathom the unimaginable pain!

We know that when Naomi decided to return to her homeland, she released her daughters-in-law to stay in their new homeland. Orpah agreed, but the bond between Ruth and Naomi prevented Ruth from ever wanting to be without her. Instead, Ruth took the lead in determining to remain together, travel together and live out the remainder of her life close to the one who had shared the same loss of spouse and security. While it may not have been a position of leadership per se, it was a journey to her "corner." What lay ahead was of little consequence as long as she and Naomi journeyed together. She decided to leave behind her past to follow a living God—Naomi's God. This singular decision enabled her to eventually realize untold blessings beyond her "corner." (Stay tuned. This gets exciting!) Naomi didn't ask Ruth to go with her, but do you think she delighted in her decision? I think so, deep down. No one wants to be alone. Ruth saw Naomi's heart and knew she **needed** to follow her. Even though

Naomi released Ruth, Ruth **wanted** to be with her, to follow her God, to continue to be part of her life. Ruth 1:16 records her reply as Naomi tried to get both daughters-in-law to return to their husbands' families and at least live around people they knew. "Where you go, I will go, and where you stay, I will stay. Your people will be my people and your God my God." In Ruth's mind and heart, there was no debating the issue. Her heart was settled on being with Naomi.

Just a little humor for a point of illustration. Every Mother's Day we hear mothers saying things like, "Oh, you don't have to get me anything . . ." Right? Wrong! We say it but we don't mean it. We want something from the heart, not some token text message or call late at night just before midnight. I think Naomi really wanted Ruth to follow her back to her people. I think it made her heart pound with delight when Ruth made it public that there would be no turning back for her—onward and upward to life's newest adventure! If we look at the relational connection between the two, it had begun years ago when Ruth was first noticed by Naomi's son. The rest is history. Now, it's Naomi and Ruth. Two women together, thrust into a most dangerous dilemma as they began their journey to their providential "corner."

There are times in our lives when everything takes a turn and things once experienced never again resurface. It's like turning onto a superhighway from a dirt road. We go from making slow progress on a bumpy road to really making progress on a smooth and well-maintained thoroughfare. Those times when everything takes on a different meaning and perspective are called "defining moments." They are moments that not only define us, but define our journey, rate of travel, and ultimate destination. They are pivotal forks in the road that eventually bring us to the exact place the Father wants us to be. After all, He's working a plan that not only includes us, but makes us major players.

Ruth's proclamation to follow Naomi became one of several moments in her life when God proved that He knew the end from the beginning in the life of an obedient child. To be certain, the death of her husband and the forced decisions she had to make became the "forks in the road" that would determine outcomes that made it possible for humanity to have a saving hope *and* a savior. More later.

The chapter on "Defining Moments" in John Maxwell's book, The 21 Irrefutable Laws of Leadership, provides three types of defining moments. These moments resonate with each of us as we can identify specific times and places in which our destiny turned from hopelessness to hopefulness. Maxwell calls the first of these "moments," **Heartbreakers**. The very word connotes a type of destruction of our emotional center—our heart. These heartbreaker moments usually happen suddenly and prevent us from any kind of preparation or positive self-talk. They just happen. We are left to pick the shattered pieces of our lives without any advance warning. The pain associated with these events takes us to the end of our tolerance with the thresholds of emotional pain and distress. I have watched as those left reeling from a tragic loss simply had to learn to put one foot in front of the other as they forced themselves to re-enter life and deal with the indescribable sense of aloneness.

When the three women's husbands die, there is triple the amount of pain and loss. Ironically, none of them could say, "I'm the only one going through this." They shared the pain and grief as all had to decide the way forward. Most likely, each even questioned their faith in what or whomever they believed. While we cannot know the extent of their disappointment, I am fairly certain that their pain was the same pain felt by those today who lose their spouse to tragedy or illness.

An event that caused me to question my faith took place in a town where we planted a thriving church then had to watch as it fell victim to the economic collapse of the 1980's. There were over seven thousand foreclosures of homes in our area. Among other disappointments and my depression, we came within two weeks of losing the dream home we built with our own hands while my husband worked bi-vocationally to provide for our young family. Neither he nor I could rationalize or explain what had taken place. We only knew that our faith was at an all-time low and that God had apparently deserted us.

It was during this particular time in our lives that we experienced the Heartbreaker moment when we had to sell the house for just enough to break even. How was God going to fix this!? Looking back at the event from today's box seats, we realize that neither one of us died and we both grew to trust God more than we thought possible. In retrospect, we did not lose any money on our house, either. The amount we thought we had lost came back to us on a later home sale in which we made a tidy gain.

We could each make a list of things and events we considered Heartbreakers. At the time, they sucked all the air right out of our lives. We were left wondering if we could ever recover. I need to offer a warning here. If we are not careful, heartbreakers can literally immobilize us from moving forward. They have a way of robbing us of any faith and we get stuck in unbelief. The good news is that when we cry out to God, He hears us! He does not evaluate our cry on the basis of eloquence or merit. He hears our heart and feels our pain. He is faithful—even when we are guilty of blaming Him for catastrophes or tragedies. He knows the human heart and He will not give weight to negative comments we make during those heartbreaker moments.

A second type of "defining moment" is the **Groundbreaker** moment. When I think of groundbreaking, I think of gardening or farming where the rocky hard ground has to be tilled and turned-up to prepare it for the seed. Likewise, the Groundbreaking of our lives is when God digs deep to uncover the lies we believe—to get below the surface or pull away the veneer so He can replace it with His Truth. Just think of Ruth. Her husband had died, and she was left without an identity or security. She had to let go of the past and follow the Living God! She also chose to follow Naomi into an unknown future.

Are you **stuck** in the Heartbreaker moment of your life? Have you let go of the hurts, offenses, bitter relationships, or tragedies? You cannot experience the **Groundbreaker** moments until you decide to agree with God and realize that He is well able to take you on to a better time and place than where you have been camped since the Heartbreaker.

During a trying time in my life, I read Lisa Bevere's book, "Lioness Arising." I commend her for her insight into gaining progress when your circumstances tell you otherwise. The one point that hit me hardest was her advice to stop repeating your problems to those who will listen! There is a time and place to share our hurts, but then there is a time to let it go. We like to find others who will sympathize and massage our hurts – it feels good. Then there's a time when it morphs into self-pity. It was hard for me to accept, but I knew it was time to, as Bob Newhart said in one of his situation comedy spots in which he was counseling a fighting couple, "Stop it . . . just Stop it!"

I remember the day when the dark clouds of depression starting to gather once again. I knew what that meant. The memories of my previous struggle sounded an alarm in my spirit, and I

remembered that I had a choice. I boldly declared,
"I'm NOT going back there again!" I had gained too
much victory to willingly relinquish it to a defeating
pattern from my past. I opened my mouth to speak
life into myself one day at a time. I closed my ears to
its luring siren. As I look back on that moment when
I took a stand against the once familiar black hole, I
realized that I had developed tools to aid in my
forward movement away from the deathly seduction
of depression. I utilized the truth of God's Word to
renew my mind. I gained a psychological
understanding of my own mind and a physical
understanding of my body. And, I began to
understand how generational strongholds lure many
a hapless victim into just accepting their particular
lot in life—good or bad.

During my **Heartbreaker** moments, I
conceived all sorts of remedies that I could accept in
light of my apparent losses. I made a list and
checked it twice. But I missed one very vital
ingredient to God's intervention in my dilemma. **I
had to accept that things would not be how I
wanted them to be** but believe in the possibility
that God can change our circumstances when we
move forward anyway! My half-empty glass suddenly
became a half-full glass with promise.

Once we begin to move away from the constraints of our **Heartbreaker**, we begin to see things through spiritual eyes. It's called faith! Heb. 11:1 says, "The substance of things hoped for, the evidence of things not seen." Abraham believed God even when he didn't see or understand. Yet, God provided a venue in which he would become one of the most revered men in biblical history. In order for that to happen, he had to get past the disappointments associated with having no heirs to believing in God enough to "call those things that didn't exist as though they did." God will use the fuel from your decision to trust Him to propel you to a new level of existence. He will show you how He strategically orchestrated each event in your life to bring you precisely to the place you are today. You have had some **Groundbreakers** and you will have more. Where are you today? Do you call it bad luck or divine providence? Ruth didn't know what was ahead, but she moved forward anyway.

We discussed **Heartbreaker** moments and the inevitable chance to move past that moment in time when all seems lost. The chance to move again is called a **Groundbreaker** moment. Once a person gains traction away from their deepest life disappointment, they find themselves in an arena of possibility and promise. The third defining moment

I want to highlight is the **Chartbreaker** moment. All three moments I highlighted here are meant by God to be defining moments in which we begin to live life again, but with a whole different perspective. We begin to see and experience things we only dared to dream of just a short time ago. God's world of incredible possibilities opens up to us as we step across the threshold of His promises and His love.

Ruth's blessing was just around her "corner." She must have thought that things would get better someday, but in her culture where women were subservient to men, she probably did not linger on the "what-ifs" of misfortune turned into fortune. Right now, survival was the only thing on her social agenda and the premise of a better life seemed remote. However, God had different plans. For reasons known only to Him, He allowed her husband to die and for her to attach herself to Naomi.

During the course of the next several months, Ruth followed Naomi to Bethlehem and began to glean grain dropped by the reapers in the fields of barley. One night, Naomi told Ruth to stay close to the reapers hired by a man named Boaz. One day as she gleaned the wasted grain cast off by the reaping process, Boaz noticed her. He enquired as to who

she was and was told that she was the young
Moabite woman who came back with Naomi from
the land of Moab. They also told him that she had
asked permission to glean alongside of them and that
she was faithful to be there day after day. Here
comes the **Groundbreaker**. Boaz told Ruth to
continue gleaning barley alongside of his reapers as
he had told the young men to leave her alone. He
also gave her permission to drink from the same
water pots as did his reapers when she got thirsty.

Ruth was overwhelmed at his kindness and
did not fully understand the reason why. When she
asked him, he said, "It has been fully reported to me
all that you have done for your mother-in-law since
the death of your husband, and how you have left
your father and mother and the land of your birth,
and have come to a people you did not know before.
The Lord repay your work, and a full reward be
given you by the Lord God of Israel, under whose
wings you have come for refuge." (Ruth 2:11-12 -
NKJV) He further invited her to sit with the
harvesters and eat the same food as they ate and
drink from the same water cistern. (I can only think
of the period in our national history when blacks
were not given the same rights as whites—even
though they were no longer slaves. They were made
to drink from the "colored only" water fountain and

sit in the balcony during movies in the local theater. Thankfully, we broke the back of segregation and enjoy equal rights for all.) But back then, foreigners were not provided the same rights as nationals. Boaz told his young men to purposefully drop grain for her to glean when they returned to the fields.

The relationship between Ruth and Boaz began to develop into something special. In those days, according to their custom, a widowed woman was usually not at the top of the "look who's available" list. Rather, she was looked upon as a second-class citizen with little, if any, social standing. The custom required her to be redeemed by a man whose stature in the community was exemplary. Boaz, being a relative of Naomi, became a kinsmen-redeemer to Ruth. His redemption provided unlimited social standing and privilege. It also meant that she could also own land. Boaz became her husband and from her bloodline came King David—just three generations away.

But wait! Here it is – the **Chartbreaker** of all **Chartbreakers**! Don't miss this! Through the bloodline of David came the Messiah—Jesus, the Christ. God took a widow woman with no social standing to literally reach her "corner" where God's blessing and promise gave her an onramp to "who's

who" in Bible chronologies. God used her bloodline
to produce the promised Messiah and bring the
chance for redemption to a lost and dying world.
Please just stop and think about this for a moment!
Think about yourself and how you might have
diminished yourself, your story, or your journey into
nothingness and yet God had a plan to fulfill His
purpose in you!

Ruth and Naomi charted a course through the
tumultuous waters of uncertainty because they chose
to trust in a God who does not always reveal the
purposes for his detours in life. On the other hand,
Orpah chose to stay in her native land and take her
chances. How did she turn out? In rabbinic
literature, Orpah is identified with Herse, the mother
of the four Philistine giants, one of whom was
Goliath. These four sons were said to have been
given her for the tears which she shed at parting with
her mother-in-law (Babylonian Talmud, Sotah 42b).
Orpah's bloodline produced the Giant that David
slew with a slingshot causing a turning point in the
war between the Israelites and the Philistines.
Imagine the contrast. One sister-in-law produced a
king and a Messiah while the other produced four
giants that fought against the people of God. Orpah
never reached her "corner" of promise and will ever
be remembered as the mother to the blasphemous

giant whose life ended as a small stone imbedded itself right between his arrogant eyes at the hands of an unlikely shepherd boy who knew the source of his strength was God.

Let me encourage you to grab ahold of a verse just packed with promises about life before and after the "corner." Ephesians 3:20 says, "Now to him who is able to do immeasurably more than all we ask or imagine, according to his power that is at work within us…" When Paul the Apostle said, "more than all we ask or imagine," he erased the barriers to what we could expect from God our Father. You might say He shattered the ceiling that once kept us from seeing anything beyond our confining space of hopelessness. I will say with unalterable confidence that once God is allowed to shatter your ceiling, you will never be the same.

Everyone has a journey to their "corner." Everyone's story is different but relevant to the principles in moving forward. There are lessons to be learned and lessons to be shunned. There are strategic points along the way in which God desires to shape our character and refine our faith. We cannot arrive at the "corner" with an unregenerate and undisciplined perspective on life. In fact, our "corner" will remain elusive until the lessons in the school of the Spirit are taken to heart and applied to life.

I mentioned that I was a shy girl who would rather let someone else be the life of the party or the leader in the classroom. I loved God and just wanted to serve Him. I did not have a dream because I had been conditioned to paying attention to the real-world right in front of me. I must admit, even though I now enjoy the benefits of allowing my dream to unfold, I got a late start at giving it permission to do so. When I was young and in high school, I paid attention to getting good grades and being a good daughter to my parents. As I left for college, the journey to my "corner" began. I got married in my second year of college and began raising a family a few years later. I majored in being overwhelmed and underappreciated. My world began to close in and by the time I was in my thirties, the load of family and ministry became so burdensome that I lapsed into a deep depression. I earlier explained that depression in detail.

During the decade of my forties, I began to transition to a positive mindset and realize that I was not the only person going through this series of life's speed bumps. As I observed others entering the perilous waters of depression, I was able to share with them the hope that came to me like a life preserver and kept me from slipping beneath the surface. My positive mindset began to take on a life-changing effect on me and others with whom I shared. When someone previously had said to me, "Just hang on. God's blessings are just around the corner," I doubted if there was a corner at all. But now, I realize that my "corner" is past, and I am beginning to enjoy God's blessings—just as He had promised years earlier. The decade of our fifties found us moving to Florida as my husband accepted a position as a Regional Executive Director for our denomination. I became the national Women's Network Director and thoroughly enjoyed serving the women in our movement for ten years. I earned a master's degree in Leadership through Assemblies of God Theological Seminary and have become certified as a leadership and life coach through John Maxwell leadership organization. I spoke at numerous national and international women's' events. I found myself living my dream as I was able to relate to women going through the same questions as I had faced earlier in my life. I was able to tell them, "There IS a corner and God DOES want to bless you there." Just one thing to clarify. Once you reach your "corner," you will realize how the journey there prepared you to be able to understand the providential process God uses in shaping those He uses and how important it is to trust Him in the process.

There Had Better Be a Corner!

Chapter 6

Dealing with Irregular People

"Our spiritual journey is like refueling our spiritual person much the same way as we would refuel our car when the tank nears empty. There are no shortcuts there! One cannot simply grab a garden hose and fill the tank with water. It is the wrong liquid! Only the fuel gained from time spent with the Father will instruct us in the proper way to deal with life's difficult people."

I recall reading about "irregular people" several years ago in a book by Joyce Landorf. An **irregular person** is someone who can push all your red buttons just by being in the same room, by giving a seemingly innocent comment, or even a certain look your way. Some irregular people are **acquaintances** that you can avoid, but sometimes they are **co-workers** or **family** members and you can't run away from them. They might be your boss or someone with authority over you. They might have indirect influence over a part of your life, and you feel powerless to minimize their contact with your job or home.

There are the good news/bad news

perspectives that help shape our reaction to their influence or effect on our life. The good news is that they are not always bad people. In fact, they're probably just like us in many ways. The bad news is that their effect causes us to make poor decisions or harbor ill will that ends up causing sin in our heart. Part of that bad news is that we have to live with them in our sphere of influence and they always seem to insert a variable that wrecks the equation of what we had planned. Or, maybe it's just being around them that grates on us till we simply want to be somewhere else.

Here's another angle from which to examine the equation. Maybe WE are the irregular person and don't even know it. If we DO know it, we are unwilling (as most irregular people are) to do anything about it. It seems that presents us with a problem. Either way, we must deal with the problem of the "irregulars." They seem to be one of life's little constants that pop up like Whack-a-Moles.

The good news is that we do have some choices! Those choices shape your heart to be more grace-giving and less judgmental. Hannah was a woman in the Bible who dealt with the consummate irregular person. Her story is in your Christ-follower Owner's Manual in I Samuel 1:1-19. We usually fumble through trying to fix something before turning to the owner's manual. Even then, we hope the answer pops out at us but when it doesn't come quickly, we go to the "trouble-shooter" section! Let's see . . . What to do when the computer will not turn on: "Check to see if it is plugged in." Ah there! Problem solved. I wish dealing with irregular people were that easy. I could just unplug them! But I dare say, that Hannah did not have that choice and, as we are about to find out, we really do not either.

I once heard a pastor compare our spiritual development to our physical development. One cannot expect to see defined muscles on their body after only three days of working out. Neither can we see spiritual habits develop after only a short time. Our spiritual journey is like refueling our spiritual person much the same way as we would refuel our car when the tank nears empty. There are no shortcuts there! One cannot simply grab a garden hose and fill the tank with water. It is the wrong liquid! It will not ignite like gasoline and propel our car along its route. The same is true when dealing with our spiritual journey's "speed bumps." Only the fuel gained from time spent with the Father will instruct us in the proper way to deal with life's difficult people.

Allow me to set this biblical narrative in applicable steps that allow us to get from one place to another in dealing with difficult people. Hannah was married to a wonderful man and she loved him. There was no issue with the love part. The issue was that Hannah could not produce children for the husband she loved. End of story? No. In fact, this issue was what propelled her to consult the owner's manual for "emergency only" advice. We live in a society that frowns on a man having more than one wife at a time. But the culture in which Hannah lived allowed the husbands to have more than one wife. Even God allowed this to happen. RED FLAG! I recall my husband returning from an east Africa mission trip and telling me that during a trek into the bush country, his group often came upon what seemed to be small villages. When he asked the guide if they were villages, the guide laughed and said, "No, this man has many wives and he constructed a house for each." It was his way of saying, "You cannot have more than one wife in the kitchen. Otherwise, there would be much trouble." Imagine Hannah's dilemma. Her husband loved her but not enough to keep trying to have children with her. For him, it was like going to an empty well and trying to draw water. A woman's identity centered around having children. If there were no children, there was no honor—only shame—both public and private. Medical technology did not exist whose diagnosis would indicate who had the deficiency— the husband or wife. It was generally considered to be the wife's fault if she did not bear children.

The solution for Hannah's husband was to simply go to another "well." He chose Peninnah. She was a Fertile Myrtle and had a bunch of kids. To add insult to injury, she made Hannah endure many years of flaunting her fertility every chance she got. She was Hannah's irregular person. Peninnah. Just say that name out loud. It does not even sound like it should be a real person's name. It became like fingernails on a blackboard to Hannah. Every time she heard about Peninnah having another little brat, she cringed and withdrew deeper into her own insecurities and shame. Hannah was no longer considered the featured wife to her husband and it was as if Peninnah took everything away from her.

Hannah's husband, Elkanah, noticed this not-so-subtle conflict going on between them and decided to try to comfort Hannah. He said to her, "Aren't I worth more than ten sons?" He didn't get it. He thought that flaunting the fact that she was his wife and that she should be grateful just did not strike a comforting chord. She had enough of the flaunting with Peninnah always taking every advantage to rub it in her face that it was her and her alone that gave her husband the continuation of the family bloodline.

If you are reading this and you are a man, don't check out on me. This topic is not about infertility or motherhood or a woman's issue. It is about how we respond to situations with difficult people or circumstances in our lives and understanding why God allows it. The real question for today is, "How do we respond or how do we react to circumstances God allows in our lives?" The forgotten truth of the matter is that irregular people are not always bad people. Sometimes they are even believers. And sometimes, WE are the difficult person in someone else's struggle for social sanity. Before we can deal effectively with irregular people, we need to be honest about who needs the attitude adjustment or the proper perspective.

Vs. 4-8: "Whenever the day came for Elkanah to sacrifice, he would give portions of the meat to his wife Peninnah and to all her sons and daughters. [5] But to Hannah he gave a double portion because he loved her, and **the LORD had closed her womb.** [6] And because the LORD had closed her womb, her rival kept provoking her in order to irritate her. [7] **This went on year after year.** Whenever Hannah went up to the house of the LORD, her rival provoked her till she wept and would not eat."

Every year, Hannah's family traveled to Shiloh to worship at the temple and offer sacrifices. In Hannah's case, she had to travel with not only her husband but also with Peninnah and her children. I can imagine them running, playing, and fighting amongst themselves. In that day, there was no family station wagon or SUV. They all traveled together—mostly on foot. I can also imagine Hannah having to corral the kiddies from time to time and help keep them together as they journeyed along the path to Shiloh. After all, they were a big happy family. Right? Maybe Hannah even had nick names for each child—ones she couldn't say out-loud. But there she was—helping keep track of everyone and being constantly reminded that she still had no legacy or promise to protect. Only Peninnah's. The scripture text says it well.

> "Whenever Hannah went up to the house of the LORD, her rival provoked her till she wept and would not eat."

Peninnah's continual harassment kept Hannah worn down and depressed. Whenever she wanted,

Peninnah could push the right buttons and Hannah would again be shamed—at will. It became a cruel game that always had the same result—a crushed and helpless person falling victim to the insults and innuendos of a merciless bully.

Finally, Hannah could take no more. She ran to God, determined to be rid of the shame and ridicule experienced daily at the hand of her evil counterpart, Peninnah. She went into the temple to pray by herself. We cannot imagine the pain she felt or the fervency with which she prayed. Eli, the priest, noticed her and thought she was drunk since only her lips seemed to stammer with unheard words.

> Vs. 10-11: "**In bitterness of soul** Hannah wept much and prayed to the LORD. [11] And she made a vow, saying, "O LORD Almighty, if you will only look upon your servant's misery and remember me, and not forget your servant but give her a son, then I will give him to the LORD for all the days of his life, and no razor will ever be used on his head."

She did not know it at the time, but her promise to God was all He needed to hear from her heart. He already had plans to grant her wish, but he wanted to make sure she knew the stakes of promising her first-born to God's service. She had no idea that her son would become a very significant priest and would actually anoint a future king. Eli had been eavesdropping and God touched his heart, prompting him to give her His message. Verse 17 says,

> "Go in peace and may the God of Israel grant you what you have asked of him." She responded by saying, "May your servant find favor in your eyes."

Hannah experienced loss, grief, humiliation, shame, injustice, disappointment, unrealized expectations, dashed dreams, and daily irritation causing depression and anger. Have you been there? Each of us will, at one time or another, have to "gut up and get through" a time of social or familial stress that pushes us to the limits. Hannnah suffered in silence and apparently, only Elkanah and Peninnah knew of her on-going pain. Her husband sought to alleviate it and her adversary sought to exploit it through her continual bombardment of painful taunts.

There is a question we must all answer. Do we *respond* objectively, or do we *react* defensively to circumstances that God allows in our lives? When we react, we usually ask the question, "Whose fault is this?" We have an inherent need to attach blame to awkward or painful situations. When we attach blame to another individual, we proceed with the misguided assumption that we will be vindicated and set in the clear from all accusations levied in this instance. It's like the character from Disney's 1997 film, Rocketman, who always said, "It's not my fault. I didn't do it," before he even knew what was going on. His only concern was that he did not get blamed for things that went wrong. Hannah was in too much pain to fight back. Instead, she took her grievance to God. While Peninnah was unkind, insensitive, and obnoxious, Hannah knew that her only defense was to give her situation to God and then trust Him for the outcome. She literally gave God the satisfaction of knowing that she trusted Him. It did not mean that she would have to trust Peninnah—only God's plan for her and for her pending blessing—you know, just around "the corner."

Many people have asked why they have to put up with irregular people in their lives. Why? God allows people like that in our lives to shape us. He did not put them there just to drive us crazy. He did not put them there to change them through our influence. He put them there to show us the evil in our own hearts. They may never change. Whether they do or do not should not concern us. God seeks to get our attention on what He wants to accomplish through our lives. Other people may just be the sandpaper He uses to shape us into the image of His Son, Jesus Christ. I particularly like the picture of the potter's hands shaping the piece of malleable clay into a thing of use and beauty. Isaiah 64:8 says, "Lord, you are our Father. We are the clay; you are the potter; we are the work of your hand." Hannah most certainly felt the pressure of the potter's hand upon her life and circumstances. She, at times, bristled at the pressure and the pain of being shaped into a vessel God could use. It was all necessary because it would later serve God's purpose in shaping the whole country by producing a priest who authenticated God's plan through a king whom he would anoint as a participant in the bloodline of the Anointed One, Jesus Christ. **There was more at stake than Hannah's comfort and reputation.** This was to be an integral part of God's plan for the redemption on humankind.

As God changes us, our attention gets drawn away from having to endure irregular people to being able to discern the changes in our own perspectives that had previously shaped our hearts. My husband once observed how a man mistreated his mother and siblings by demeaning them at every chance and providing a false narrative of the whole family. My husband told me that this individual would never darken our doorstep and would never be welcome in our home. He was about to launch his own crusade to set things right and put the individual in his place. Then, God intervened and showed him the evil in his own heart—by his own admission. God literally used the individual he despised to show him how he had taken the matter out of His hands and placed it in his own. God did not need my husband to be a crusader. He needed to show him how his thoughts and potential actions would cause more harm than good and that my husband needed to repent for trying to act independently of God's process. Wow! Talk about seeing things in a different perspective! My husband would have only made things worse, not better. While his intentions were good, his plan produced sin in his heart.

We can tell when God is getting through to us. We begin to ask different questions and see different solutions to the painful process of getting aligned with God's will. What if he wants to change us, not them? Can we be thankful for them, forgive them, bless them, pray for their success? You might say, "It's just too hard!" Yes, it is. "I can't forgive." Yes, you can. Do you hear that? Yes, you can! Forgiveness literally delivers you from the bondage of a painful life episode and releases you into a season of gratefulness and emotional freedom. You will even find it possible to pray for your tormentor's success in finding the right path God designed for them.

Just look at Hannah. Was her familial pain God's fault? It is not about fault. It's about a providential plan. It was God who closed her womb. Remember, this is not only about infertility, but about God closing doors of opportunity in our lives in order to shape us and direct us to His best plan for us. Was her dilemma Satan's fault? No. In fact, we give him too much credit for the things that seem to go wrong when it is usually God who allows tests and trials to shape us into useful vessels.

When Hannah went to the temple to pray, she might have been intent upon getting God to change her circumstances. She was on the verge of bitterness. God had turned up the heat and pressure in her life, like the potter with the clay in his hands – shaping and molding. How did God change her? She became more sensitive to those in similar circumstances. When life is good, we can become judgmental. (cancer, infertility, financial loss, difficult relationship, death of loved one). But when we feel the heat, it is time to check the spiritual thermostat and allow God to change our heart. Our Scriptural passage reveals that she left her pain at the altar and went out different than how she came in. Her weight was lifted, and she began to live with an expectancy of getting past her "corner" and realizing God's richest blessing.

Hannah did three things to seal the deal with her Heavenly Father. **First,** she **suffered with dignity** – she stopped repeating the drama. She had to come to terms with the Penninah in her life. She left Peninnah at the altar. No longer would she blame her for the pain she endured.

Second, she **addressed her own anger.** Depression is anger turned inward. Instead she RAN to God! "God, you are the only one who can change this. But more important, God, change me!" Hannah realized her circumstances were intended to purify her motives. She opened her hands and released her brokenness, her lost dream, her unrealized expectations of how her life should be. She simply (and effectively) prayed. She also had to examine her motives for having children. Would that become her identity or her vengeance? Or did she want her life to bring glory to God no matter what, or did she just want to be respected as a fruitful spouse?

Third, she **sang a song.** She knew that her

barrenness was about to be a thing of the past. Not only did God give her a son she named Samuel, but she had several more children as a reward from God for her willingness to let Him have her first-born. In chapter 2 she found her identity in God, not motherhood. God did answer her prayer, **but He wanted Samuel for HIS glory.** God wanted Samuel to be born and needed to know that Hannah's heart was pure so she could release him to his destiny even as a child. Samuel was destined to become a great leader and spiritual influence in Israel.

We will experience a time in which we question everything we believe. It is not a matter of whether or not that time ever comes, it is a matter of **when** it comes. No man or woman will escape their time of tests and trials. They reveal themselves in different forms and in different "irregulars" that God, if given the chance, will use to shape us and show us that we can sing in the middle of the situation, too. We will discover that praise is a spiritual weapon that bolsters us in the midst of calamity and danger. Praise provides an on-ramp for God to start revealing the purpose for the process. Remember **Peter** in jail? His praise opened the locked door and proved to him that God was working on his behalf. He even praised God when he was near death. "From the rising of the sun, to the setting down of the same, the Lord's Name is to be praised!" In good times and in bad times, I WILL REJOICE!

APPLICATION:

- What is your Samuel, your brokenness, your disappointment? **Will your prayer bring glory to God?**

- Who is your Penninah? Will you thank God that He is using that person or situation to **form** you into His image – **even if they never change?**

- We have a choice today. We can **React** to the situation with blame, anger, vengeance, self-pity, or moodiness, or we can **Respond** by letting God mold us and set another person free!

The Father wants us to experience freedom from the things we consider painful and unfair. But He also wants to develop us into faithful and fruitful children who know His voice and trust Him in their circumstances. If you have ever watched as someone else seemingly enjoyed things that remained elusive to you, understand that your Heavenly Father knows all about you and has a very special plan for your life. It demands trusting Him and giving Him permission to, as David realized, "create in you a clean heart and renew a steadfast spirit within you." God has a special blessing for you just "around the corner." You **will** get there and you **will** consider it all worth the pain or difficulty in your journey there.

There Had Better Be a Corner!

Chapter 7

"Don't Let It Die!"

"Give your dreams back to God—especially if they seem to have suffered a premature death. God will not ruin His perfect record on your situation."

Some of the travel destinations in the fall are places where the seasons are more pronounced and produce changing leaves. Colorado is famous for the beautiful fall season. On the downside, cold weather is required to produce the most brilliant color in the leaves. Several years ago, we visited Colorado and saw just the beginning of fall there. Beautiful color radiated from the landscape and hills as we made our way to the hotel close to the church we planted in 1979. We had been invited to share in the dedication of a brand-new building the congregation and pastor built. We had pastored there 9 years, then another pastor came for 18 years. They asked us to come celebrate with them in this milestone as a church. The pastor who succeeded us was very gracious as he presented us as the founding pastors of the church. As I mentioned in a previous chapter, the church-plant undertaking was very hard on us as a family and in our marriage. Lots of memories flooded back in during that trip. It represented a "season" of our lives. It was a season of faith – church planting, raising three sons, and my husband being bi-vocational. But now, we could look back on it and realized that God really did keep good books. He is the one who balances the ledger and keeps things above water.

While that experience drudged up some painful memories, it was necessary for us to see just how deep the pain had been and how completely God brought us through our times of despair and depression. Our church plant was successful, and we survived a myriad of personal feelings and experiences. I think God just wanted us to see that in spite of our perception of things, He was faithful to accomplish what He desired—even though we felt we had failed.

Just before we left that town and moved our family to Iowa, God gave us a glimpse into our future. Normally, I give little credence to "words of prophecy" given by those claiming to be prophets. This particular individual was a friend of ours whom we recognized as having prophetic gifts. He had called earlier and asked if he could come by and see

us since he was in town visiting family in Denver.
We welcomed the opportunity to him again and
perhaps speak something into our lives since the
previous year had us on the sidelines working secular
jobs and wondering if God was finished with our
service to Him. Our ministry had taken a toll on us.
We rested for a year and were ready to push on to
whatever God wanted—as long as it was truly Him
talking to us. We trusted our friend as someone
capable of hearing from God and obedient enough
to tell us what he perceived God to be saying at this
juncture in our lives.

He was low-key and deliberate as we sat
together at our kitchen table. He began to make a
diagram on a piece of typing paper. As he moved
along, his diagram started to resemble the rock
formation seen from the interstate at the north end
of Castle Rock. It's the reason the town was named
Castle Rock. It's a long story, but he did not know
he was drawing the rock because his diagram was
upside down to him. As he progressed, we sat there
just staring at his artwork and having a confirmation
from God develop as he drew. This would not mean
anything to anyone else. In fact, most would say we
only saw what we *wanted* to see. Like they say, you
would have to have been there. Then he delivered
these words that he sensed were God's message to

us: "I will make you a pastor to pastors and a teacher to teachers. You will have more impact than you ever imagined. God has a plan for you and that's why He's taking you through these rough times. He's training you for your next assignment." We certainly did not feel like we had faith for that or anything else. We felt forgotten!

As he spoke, we wept—partially because he was telling us that God was not finished with us and that his words were really zeroing in on questions we held in our hearts. **We felt our dream of doing something significant for God had died.** He was telling us that God was about to resurrect our passion and redirect it in another area.

My husband was reluctant to allow God to guide us through another ministry valley. He saw the impact it had on our little family and had worked midnights to provide food and clothing for the boys and myself. But I could see the light come on in his eyes as our friend shared with us about the "mission impossible" that lay ahead of us. We only had to be obedient and trust God to open the doors He wanted us to go through. That was thirty years ago. We still hold that encounter with our friend and God as pivotal in our ongoing service to our heavenly Father.

Scripture records another story of a dream dying and then being raised to life. It is found in 2 Kings 4:8-37 (NLT). I like this version's rendering of this story. As you read the story, make these replacements: The Shunammite woman represents you and me. Elisha represents God. The Boy represents God's promises via prophecies to us. You will be amazed at how personal this becomes for you.

> [8] One day Elisha went to Shunem. An important woman was there, who talked him into eating some food. So, every time he passed by, he would turn in there to eat food. [9] She said to her husband, "Now I see that this is a holy man of God who is always passing by. [10] Let us make a little room on the second floor. And let us put a bed there for him, and a table and a chair and a lamp. Then when he comes to us, he can go in there."

> [11] One day Elisha came there and went into the room on the second floor and rested. [12] He said to Gehazi his servant, "Call this Shunammite." When he had called her, she came and stood in front of him. [13] Elisha said to Gehazi, "Now tell her, 'See, you have done much for us. What can I do for you?

Should I speak to the king or to the captain of the army for you?'" And she answered, "I live among my own people." [14] So Elisha said, "What then is to be done for her?" Gehazi answered, "She has no son, and her husband is old." [15] Elisha said, "Call her." When he had called her, she stood at the door. [16] Then he said, "At this time next year you will hold a son in your arms." And she said, "No, my lord, O man of God. Do not lie to your woman servant." [17] Later she was going to have a child and she gave birth to a son at that time the next year, as Elisha had told her. [18] When the child was grown, he went out one day to his father who was with those gathering grain. [19] He said to his father, "O, my head, my head!" The father said to his servant, "Carry him to his mother." [20] When he was brought to his mother, he sat on her knees until noon. Then he died. [21] She went up and laid him on the bed of the man of God. She shut the door behind him and went out. [22] Then she called to her husband and said, "Send me one of the servants and one of the donkeys, that I may run to the man of God and return." [23] Her husband said, "Why will you go to him today? It is not the time of the new moon or the Day of Rest." She said, "It will be all right." ²⁴ Then she put a seat on a donkey and said to her servant, "Drive on. Do not slow down for me unless I tell you." ²⁵ So she went and came to the man of God at Mount Carmel. When the man of God saw her far away, he said to Gehazi his servant, "See, there is the Shunammite. ²⁶ Run now to meet her. Say to her, 'Is it well with you? Is it well with your husband? Is it well with the child?'" And she answered, "It is well." ²⁷ When she came to the mountain to the man of God, she took hold of his feet. Gehazi came near to push her away, but the man of God said, "Let her alone. For her soul is troubled within her. The Lord has hidden it from me. He has not told me." ²⁸ Then she said, "Did I ask you for a son? Did I not say, 'Do not lie to me'?"

²⁹ Elisha said to Gehazi, "Get ready to travel. Take my walking stick and go. If you meet any man, do not greet him. If anyone greets you, do not answer him. Then lay my stick on the boy's face." ³⁰ The mother of the boy said, "As the Lord lives and as you yourself live, I will not leave you." So, Elisha got up and followed her. ³¹ Gehazi went on before them

and laid the stick on the boy's face. But there was no sound or anything to show that the boy was alive. So Gehazi returned to meet Elisha, and told him, "The boy is not awake." [32] When Elisha came into the house, he saw the boy lying dead on his bed. [33] So he went in and shut the door behind the two of them and prayed to the Lord. [34] He went up and lay on the child. He put his mouth on his mouth, and his eyes on his eyes, and his hands on his hands. He spread himself out on him, and the child's flesh became warm. [35] Then Elisha got up again. He walked from one end of the house to the other. Then he went up and spread himself on the child again. The boy sneezed seven times and opened his eyes. [36] Elisha called Gehazi and said, "Call this Shunammite." So, he called her. When she came to him, he said, "Take up your son." [37] She came and fell at his feet and put her face to the ground. Then she took up her son and went out.

This account of the Shunammite woman resonates to all who have had a dream only to see it die. For her, she did not ask for a child. Elisha told her she would have a child, but she thought he was being cruel with her since her husband was old. Her acts of kindness to the prophet and his companion did not go unnoticed. The account says that she petitioned her husband to build an extra room for the prophet so that when he came through the region, he would have a place to stay. The gesture of **building an extra room** to her house represents sowing seeds for miracles. She was increasing her capacity for God. She didn't even know why she was being kind to the man of God—only that she was obedient to do what God had placed into her heart. We can walk out our faith by sowing seeds intentionally. I realize that some current "theology" often promotes just saying your desires aloud until God provides them. That is not what I am saying here. In fact, she did not even hold the possibility of having a child before the prophet told her she would conceive and have a son. She did not ask for a child. Yet, it was God's way of looking deep into her heart and revealing a long-lost hope of bearing children. He saw through her verbal defenses and reached the heart of the matter—she would have the child she long desired. Only God can put something like that together. Her unsuspecting part was simply to be kind to the man of God. God saw her generous heart and did the rest.

You have secret desires. You hold things in your heart that you either feel unworthy to request or do not believe possible. Have they died, been stolen, forgotten, or gone dormant? God knows what they are. He's reminding you of them today. Your present state might be one of hopelessness. You gave up on the impossible. You believe it might happen for someone else, but not you—for a variety of reasons. I can only point you to Ezekiel 37 where God set the prophet down in a valley of dry bones and asked him whether or not they could live. Ezekiel said, "You know if that is possible." God told him to prophesy to the bones. What had been hopeless and impossible became a reality. The narrative records that the bones and tissues came together and became a great army. (I think I can see this in some science fiction rendering of the army of the dead coming to life to serve a dead king.)

Pay close attention. The Shunammite woman experienced a devastating loss when her son drops dead from a pain in his head. Scripture does not say it was heatstroke or anything other than he complained to his father that his head hurt, so his father sent him to his mother. He sat on his mother's knees for a few hours then died. She arranged to get the man of God to her home as quickly as possible. When Elisha's servant, Gehazi, saw her, he asked her if everything was alright. She simply said, "Fine." But when she got to the prophet, she told him the whole story—including the part of how she **did not ask** for the child and that it was **cruel** to give him to her and then let him die. Her tunnel vision kicked in. As most mothers would, she had grown close to her son and recognized him as a gift from God. Wondering why God took him away from her was more painful than actually losing him. It became a faith issue that culminated in her righteous indignation toward this seemingly cruel act by God. Wait for it. Ah, she became deliberate enough to let God set this thing right. She hadn't given up. She was simply stating her case like it says to do in Isaiah 43:28.

We have a great deal to learn from this woman. Once she accepted God's gift to her of a son she didn't verbally request, she would not let him go so easily. She knew what she had to do, and she was willing to move heaven and earth to make it happen. She didn't talk to others about her secret desires. She went directly to God. She modeled the necessary steps to take when we do not understand our circumstances. Go directly to God – Do not pass Go! Do not post it on social media and expect an answer. Do not use it as a means to gain sympathy in a prayer meeting. If you share your dilemma with anyone, make sure they are not the church gossip or someone you cannot trust with such an important petition. The moment you just put it out there in the wind, you immediately inject **human remedy** into a situation **only** God can heal.

Give your dreams back to God—especially if they seem to have suffered a premature death. God will not ruin His perfect record on your situation. He is faithful. Has God permitted you to see your dreams, but it seems to have faded away into oblivion? He will breathe new life into them and revive them. Replace your despair with declarations of promises from the Bible: "God, **You said**, 'My grace is sufficient' – I need it now!" "God, **You said**, 'I will never leave you' – Where are you now?" That's right. Get some passion cooking! God wants to see if you mean business. If you do, nothing is impossible for Him and you will be surprised just how easily He answers.

Now get bold, take your desires and promises directly to God and speak life into them. God told Isaiah to "remind me—state your case, that you may be acquitted." Ezekiel spoke to the valley of dry bones. Bang! God showed up and blew the doors off conventional theology.

Psalm 66: 10-12 and 16-20 says, [10] "For You have tested us, O God. You have made us pure like silver is made pure. [11] You brought us into the net.

And You laid a heavy load on our back. [12] You made men travel over our heads. We went through fire and through water. But You brought us out into a place where we have much more than we need. [16] Come and hear, all who fear God, and I will tell you what He has done for me. [17] I cried to Him with my mouth and praised Him with my tongue. [18] The Lord will not hear me if I hold on to sin in my heart. **[19] But it is sure that God has heard. He has listened to the voice of my prayer.** [20] Honor and thanks be to God! **He has not turned away from my prayer** or held His loving-kindness from me."

You can be certain of one thing. God has a plan for your life. I mentioned that our friend came to our home in Colorado and spoke what he perceived to be God's word to us. I said that was thirty years ago. Since then, both my husband and I have been in national leadership roles for our denomination, earned our graduate degrees, and become a pastor to pastors and a teacher to teachers. My husband's books deal with leadership issues and have been translated into Spanish and Chinese. I became a leadership coach and regularly conduct training sessions designed to help build teams that function together as a cohesive unit. We both marvel at what God accomplished despite our earlier misgivings about whether or not He could use us again. Our dream seemed lost. We were willing to just let it die and get secular jobs, but that was not God's plan.

I hope that you will take these words seriously and allow God to resurrect your dream. He wants so much more for you than you have ever imagined. Go ahead. Try to prove Him wrong. When you are done trying, He will take what you give Him and bless it beyond your wildest imagination. It was God who put that dream in your heart in the first place. He used your imagination and faith to construct a mental facsimile of what He wants to do with and through your life. What are you waiting for? God began a good work in you. According to Philippians 1:6, "You can be **confident** that He will complete the work He started in you."

John Maxwell's book, "The 15 Invaluable Laws of Growth," he cites the example of how Sue Enquist, coach of UCLA women's softball team for 17 years, espoused the 33 Percent Rule. She said you can divide people almost anywhere into three categories—the bottom, middle and top thirds. "The bottom third suck the life out of you because nothing is ever good enough for them. The middle third is happy and positive when things are going well, but down in times of adversity. The top third maintains a positive attitude even in tough times. They are leaders, influencers, and game-changers." Every situation in our lives has been designed by God to give us a free-will choice to live in one of those three categories.

God gave us all we need to live in hope. I love the Voice rendering of Romans 12:9-14. Notice especially what it says about hope.

> "Love others well, and don't hide behind a mask; love authentically. Despise evil; pursue what is good as if your life depends on it. Live in true devotion to one another, loving each other as sisters and brothers. Be first to honor others by putting them first. Do not slack in your faithfulness and hard work. Let your spirit be on fire, bubbling up and boiling over, as you serve the Lord. Do not forget to rejoice, **for hope is always just around the corner**. Hold up through the hard times that are coming and devote yourselves to prayer. Share what you have with the saints, so they lack nothing; take every opportunity to open your life and home to others. If people mistreat or malign you, bless them."

We have no shortage of Bible study aids and tools available to us in almost any city anywhere. I found a list of declarations in BibleStudyTools.com. It's a comparison of what we say and what God says (backed up by a Scripture reference). You will find it comforting to know that God has already covered any dilemma you might face through the course of your life. He paid a great price for you to be in the "top third." You dare not discard His provision nor His promise! It is His will for you to live in victory. That is not aberrant theology. That is what He says in His Word.

If, like the Shunammite woman, you had a dream that came to life only to die, be encouraged. Hope is just around the corner. Your blessing is just around the corner. Your victory is just around the corner. Do not give up. Press on and declare God's promises—not to mean what YOU want them to mean, but to mean what GOD really meant. While you strain to get to your "corner," remember that He's not waiting around the corner for you—He's right **beside** you during your journey. He is faithful and will not let you fall along the way. Reach out and take His hand. Like I once said, "There had BETTER be a corner," it was only when I took His hand and trusted him for the journey that I found the "corner" AND the blessing and hope He had waiting for me.

Use this handy list as a quick reminder of His provision for living in that top category mentioned by Coach Enquist.

You Say	God says	Bible Verse
I can't figure it out.	I will direct your steps.	Proverbs 3:5-6
I'm too tired.	I will give you rest.	Mathew 11:28-30
It's impossible.	All things are possible.	Luke 18:27
Nobody loves me.	I love you.	John 3:16
I can't forgive myself.	I forgive you.	Romans 8:1
It's not worth it.	It will be worth it.	Romans 8:28
I'm not smart enough.	I will give you wisdom.	1 Cor. 1:30
I'm not able.	I am able.	2 Cor. 9:8
I can't go on.	My grace is sufficient.	2 Cor. 12:9
I can't do it.	You can do all things.	Phil. 4:13
I can't manage.	I will supply all your needs.	Phil. 4:19
I'm afraid.	I have not given you fear.	2 Tim. 1:7
I feel all alone.	I will never leave you.	Hebrews 13:5

There Had Better Be a Corner!

ABOUT THE AUTHOR

Kris Beaird was born in Newcastle, Wyoming, and grew up in Rapid City, South Dakota. She and her husband, Jim, have been leaders in ministry for 48 years as pastors, leaders and mentors. In 2010, she earned a Masters' Degree in ministry leadership where she was introduced to the coaching process. In 2015, she joined the John Maxwell team and became certified as a coach, speaker and trainer. The coaching process has ignited a passion within her to help those who want to maximize their potential. Her extensive cross-cultural experience nationally and internationally has enriched her immensely! Kris speaks at leadership functions and actively invests in initiatives to build leaders capable of connecting with the next generation to build further value into her team members and others. Kris is married to Jim and they have 3 grown, married sons with seven grandchildren. They live in the Tampa Bay area of Florida.